D0987423

INTERCULTURAL
MARRIAGE
Promises & Pitfalls

INTER-CULTURAL MARRIAGE

Promises & Pitfalls

Dugan Romano

intercultural press, inc.

Library of Congress Catalog No. 88-081393
ISBN 0-933662-71-8
Copyright © 1988 Dugan Romano
Published by Intercultural Press, Inc.
All rights reserved.
Printed in the United States of America.

No part of this book may be used or reproduced in any
manner whatsoever without written prior permission except
in the case of brief quotations embodied in critical articles or
reviews.

For information, contact
Intercultural Press
P.O. Box 700
Yarmouth, Maine 04096

Library of Congress Cataloging-in-Publication Data

Romano, Dugan.
    Intercultural marriage.

    Bibliography: p.
        1. Intercountry marriage.   2. Intermarriage.
I. Title.
HQ1032.R66   1988   306.8'45   88-81393
ISBN 0-933622-71-8

For Nika and Kevin
the best part of it all.

TABLE OF CONTENTS

Part 3
Making Miracles Isn't Easy

Bibliography

ACKNOWLEDGEMENTS

When a book is finally finished, it is easy to think of it as entirely one's own creation but I know that this book would never have been written without the forthright enthusiasm and honesty of the many spouses who shared with me their experiences and their thoughts and feelings about their own intercultural marriages, and whose stories form the backbone of this book; without the moral support of those friends who knew it would become a reality (even when I had some doubts); without the patience and backing of all the editors at Intercultural Press who painstakingly drew out the best from me and polished my manuscript until it reached its present state.

I want to thank my friends in Milan who shared some of the early years with me, especially Barbara Cocchini, Diane Saa, Lucy ben Fadhl, and also Julie Gavazzi-Dunn who first helped us sort it all out and who we will miss.

I want to thank Diane Zeller who kept prompting and promoting from behind the scenes in Washington, D.C. and Peggy Pusch who, together with David Hoopes and Judy Carl Hendrick, ably guided and edited me through three years of work, letting me talk out some of the glitches and assisting me in smoothing out the others.

I want to especially thank my children who understood why dinner was sometimes burned—as Mommy hovered over her word processor—and were with me all the way.

Dugan Romano
Spring, 1988
Washington, D.C.

INTRODUCTION

What's It All About?

The bride and groom were on their way: their bags packed, passports renewed, tickets and boarding passes ready.

The car taking them to the airport was surrounded by a few intimate friends, who were jovial but, at the same time, teary-eyed and cautious in their well-wishing. There were no relatives, no parents to bless these two young people and send them on their way.

The bride, flushed and smiling through her nervousness and excitement, was struggling to control the mixed sensations of happiness and hurt which were gripping her insides and jumbling everything around.

This was really a good-bye. She was leaving these people and turning her back on her family who disapproved of the marriage. She was crossing a bridge: not only the symbolic bridge that every bride crosses, but also a physical bridge to a new life in a different country, among new people with foreign ways and tongues.

Her groom, a handsome, dark-eyed, dark-skinned recent MBA graduate was finally beginning to relax. He was glad the ceremony was over and he could escape from the ambivalence of the situation.

He was anxious to return home, to the familiar atmosphere of his own land and friends. For the moment he managed to suppress the nagging fears and doubts he felt about taking this delicate, blond, blue-eyed French beauty back with him. He hoped she would win the hearts of all, just as she had won his, and that all the protestations over this marriage to a foreign woman would subside as soon as they met her.

These two young people, Yvette and Ali, one French, the other Kuwaiti, were embarking on more than the usual matrimonial adventure: they were heading into the never-never land of intercultural marriage.[1]

Carried away by the impetuosity of youth and half-comprehended dreams of romance and glamour, Yvette and Ali had few doubts about the success of their venture. They knew that their marriage might be harder than one between people from the same background, but in their hearts they were sure they would make it. They were confident that love and luck would win out over any obstacles they might encounter. For now, all they felt were the positive aspects of their international partnership. They were proud of being different, of their daring, and excited about the adventure ahead. Only later, when the honeymoon was over and they began to tame their adventure into a life together, did they realize that they had done more—much more—than marry someone with an exotic accent.

Yvette and Ali are but two of the growing number of young people crossing cultures to find lifetime partners. More and more, people are leaving their homelands to visit, study, or work overseas. Once upon a time the intercultural couple was more unusual. Young people did not have as much opportunity to meet prospective partners from other lands. But, now, distances are no longer barriers; many local customs and traditions are giving way to an apparent uniformity. Blue jeans, Coca-Cola, television series, and rock music have been adopted by young people everywhere. The whole world shares the same threats and problems—terrorism, drugs, nuclear war, poverty, pollution—and seems to be an extended global village with only superficial differences.

But actually these similarities often merely disguise the fundamental diversity in beliefs and behaviors which makes each culture unique, its people distinct.

In the early stages of all love relationships—and intercultural relationships are no exception—people are aware of and

---

[1] By which we mean a union of two people from diverse cultures as well as different countries which may also, but not necessarily, indicate differences in race and/or religion.

encouraged by the similarities between them. Any differences they do see are often disregarded as (1) surface details, (2) challenges or (3) aspects which make the relationship more interesting.

Only later, when they get down to the business of forming a cohesive, functional family unit do they realize that these differences complicate matters and have to be dealt with one way or another: accepted when possible, resolved when necessary, but not ignored. It is then that they become fully aware of how many differences there are, how deeply embedded some of them are, and how these differences are going to affect their future together.

That is when the give-and-take which is necessary to any marriage becomes important. It is also when these couples realize that for them it is also more complicated than for people in monocultural marriages, because they often don't know what, or how much, they should give and take, or why.

They are in new territory. Their differences are often based on expectations, assumptions and convictions neither one had been consciously aware of having because they were bred into them, never before questioned, obvious and yet often incomprehensible to their partners. Each spouse first has to learn a lot about him- or herself, as an individual and as a member of a culture, and then about the partner. Only then can they begin to know how to handle their differences and make them work *for* them instead of *against* them.

This can be a long, possibly a lifetime, process, and many couples don't know where to begin. They don't know where culture leaves off and person begins.

With this book we hope to help intercultural couples recognize the differences for what they are and to see them in perspective so that they can handle them to their mutual advantage. This is a book written for couples who are involved in relationships with someone from a different culture—who are either already married or are considering marriage.

It is for those of you who have come to see that your relationship/marriage is not exactly what you had fantasized, who have perhaps run into the first pitfalls and have begun to question whether you made (or are making) the right decision, whether it is worth it or not, and to wonder, "Where do we go from here?"

This book is for those couples who perhaps have had no one to turn to with their questions because they know no one who has had the same experience, couples who feel they are alone because they married against everyone's advice and now must take the consequences.

Until now there has been little written on the subject (see bibliography). Such couples have had to find their own way, often groping blindly, never sure when the things which are troubling them are typical of all marriages or unique to their own *because of* the cultural differences between the spouses.

For many of you there is no one with whom you can compare notes or share impressions of marriage because your own situation is different from others, and perhaps this differentness isolates you and sometimes intensifies your feelings of aloneness or strangeness.

With this book we hope to fill that void by (1) giving a brief overview of what makes these marriages different, special, or unique, and by explaining why they seem (are) harder than others; (2) showing where the potential troublespots (problems or challenges) are for most couples; and (3) offering some suggestions for managing the differences and making them work for, rather than against, the marriage.

To do this we are using the personal stories, ideas and advice of the hundreds of couples interviewed, some of whom have basically sound marriages, some who feel they do not, some who are still groping for the answers, and some who seem to have found them.

It is not meant to be a book with all the answers, nor one which covers every aspect of intercultural marriage, but rather, a handbook which will explore, pose a lot of questions for consideration, and lead each of you to find your own answers for your own relationships.

The overview focuses on the *kinds* of people who marry into other cultures. Here we consider some of the general personality types who are likely to marry out of their own cultures and some underlying motivations for their marriages.

We will outline the usual progress of these marriages, as couples pass from the "honeymoon" stage, when the atmosphere is optimistic and the emphasis is on all the similarities which exist between them, to the "settling-in" stage, when they get down to the basics of daily life, i.e., forming their routines, projecting their future and seeking a marital style which works for both of them.

The settling-in stage is when a couple really comes to grips with the many different ways in which each partner approaches life and discovers that some of their differences cause confusion and friction. This stage is the one in which the little habits of each partner must be adjusted to suit living as a couple.

For the intercultural couple this stage is often like going through culture shock, or the psychological disorientation similar to that experienced by people living in foreign lands, but more severe and comprehensive because of the totality of their commitment—for them there is no "going home."

The second part of the book examines the troublespots, the differences that become issues. We will look into differences which the majority of the couples interviewed felt were the most troublesome. First we will attempt to distinguish between differences stemming from ethnic or cultural origin and those which might be common to *any* marriage (personality, age, social status, educational level)—often a very fine line. We will then concentrate on the cultural differences and examine each one in depth to see *how* and *why* they cause problems in these marriages.

Lastly, the book focuses on ways of turning the differences into pluses by separating the issues from the love relationship, and seeing these issues as challenges to be managed to the couple's benefit, thereby overcoming some of the problems they might cause. We'll look at different kinds of intercultural marital arrangements, how couples have worked out their particular balance of power, and how they have resolved differences.

We will also consider some of the factors for success in these marriages and the conditions which must exist before the marriages can begin to function well, many of which apply to any marriage and some of which are specific to intercultural marriages. Finally we will give practical pointers which should be taken into consideration before marriage, as well as points to think about in case the marriage ends because of death, forced separation or divorce.

Any marriage is like a game (a very serious game); but intercultural marriage is a more complicated one because both partners come equipped with a different set of rules, by which we mean different values, habits, and viewpoints, different ways of relating to one another, and different ways of resolving their differences. Until one set of "house rules" is agreed upon, the game doesn't work, and the partners risk growing apart rather than together. Deciding on which (or whose) rules, even deciding how to decide, can be complicated and can cause misunderstandings, conflicts or ruptures, even for two people who love each other.

Although we may appear to have opened a Pandora's box, we hope that this book will serve to direct you, the reader, towards appreciating that intercultural marriage, while not for the weak of spirit, can provide incomparable opportunities for experiencing not only personal expansion, but for finding a love and closeness more special *because of* the extra effort it takes. By seeing the pitfalls, avoiding some and coping with others, I hope that each of you will find what your marriage promised… and more.

INTERCULTURAL MARRIAGE
Promises & Pitfalls

DARING
TO BE
DIFFERENT

PART 1

THE WHOS AND WHYS

Before looking at these marriages to understand why some succeed and others fail (or merely set endurance records), we must look at who the people are who cross international boundaries to find their partners. Obviously, not every person who lives and loves overseas comes back with a bride or groom. And so, who does? Who are the people who veer from the norm? What is it that distinguishes them from others?

Take a moment to think about yourself and your spouse and ask yourself honestly what it was that drew you into a permanent relationship with someone from another land. Was it chance? Coincidence? Fate? A matter of being in the right place at the right time? Or was it something within?

Here are a few other questions which might assist you in discovering the *why* of your marriage:

1.   What was it that attracted you to one another in the first place, i.e., what was the most appealing characteristic about that particular person and about the whole idea of marrying a foreigner (romance? prestige? adventure?)?

2.   How would you describe yourself in appearance and personality, at the time of the marriage: secure?

3

mature? outgoing? shy, naive, lacking in self-esteem? conformist or independent? nationalistic or not particularly patriotic? a loner or joiner? physically attractive (to the opposite sex) or not particularly appealing?

3.	What was going on in your life at the time you met: what events, situations or changes? It might be useful to look over a list of life events considered to be stress causers to see if any apply. These might include such things as deaths, marriages or births in the immediate family or circle of friends, job changes, moves to a new city, country, etc.[2]

4.	How did you feel about people from other lands or about other ethnic groups within your own country? Did you see cultures as more or less equal, or did you consider your own to be superior, or at least the one which did things in the most natural way, and, therefore, did you tend to rate the others according to their approximation to your own?

5.	What kind of relationships existed at home—with parents, siblings, peers? Were you the only or eldest child of the family?[3] What was your home life like? Was yours a close-knit unit in which one member's affairs or problems were taken on by the entire family, or was it a more disjointed kind of family in which each member went his or her own way and respected the independence and privacy of the others? Was this style right for you? Was it similar to that of most of the people you know? Was there anything in your parents' marital relationship that

[2] See *Future Facts* by Seven Rosen, pp 224-26, for a more complete listing of stress-causing life changes.

[3] Edwin H. Friedman, Family Center, Georgetown University Medical School and Family Training, Saint Elizabeth's Hospital, Washington, D.C., found that Jews who married non-Jews were almost always the oldest sibling or only child or "triangled" child in the family. See "The Myth of the Shiksa," *Ethnicity and Family Therapy*, pp 504-06.

you wanted to avoid repeating in your own? Was there a desire to get away from something (family situation, poverty, war, discrimination, personal problem)? What did you consider to be the best/ worst part about your own country, your own social, racial, religious group, or the physical or economic environment in which you lived?

6. What were your expectations regarding life with the man/woman you married, your goals for the relationship? How did your views compare or differ from your partner's? Were they compatible?

At this point we are going to briefly describe seven types of people who enter intercultural marriages—people who share certain personality tendencies or matrimonial motives—and we will group them under these general headings:

1. Outcasts

2. Rebels

3. Mavericks

4. Compensators

5. Adventurers

6. Escapists

7. Unstables

Of course, there is no one profile which exactly describes any intercultural spouse—there are too many variables, too many individuals. Most people fall into more than one category or see parts of themselves in all of them.

Behind the types and the motives, there is also timing, chance and availability. People marry when they are ready to marry—physically, psychologically, and perhaps economically. People also marry people with whom they fall in love. When considering love as a motive, however, it must be kept in mind that love may mean different things to different people.

Outcasts

Classic outcast personality types, for one reason or another, don't fit or can't make it in their own society and either feel, or actually are, ostracized by it. When they fall in love and marry people from another culture, it is often an unconscious attempt to find a place where they can belong. On occasion they choose someone from a society whose cultural norms are more compatible with their own personal norms. Sometimes they find someone who they think (because of his or her foreignness) won't *know* that they are outsiders in their own society. They see a way out of their social trap into acceptance in another society, i.e., a way of belonging somewhere.

There are any number of reasons why these people may be (or feel like) outcasts. They may be men or women who feel physically unattractive or, for some reason, unpopular with members of the opposite sex in their own group, who suddenly revel in the success they have with foreign men or women. One extremely small, slight, Western man, who was mortified by his stature and felt out of place, was overwhelmed by the success he had with Asian women. A modest, shy, homeloving virgin who hid her virtues from her actively feminist companions for fear of being ridiculed, felt that she had finally found her place when she met a man from a society in which these characteristics were admired.

Some outcasts belong to a minority race or ethnic group, are segregated from the majority, and hope to escape the prejudice which dominates their lives by marrying someone from a culture in which these particular prejudices don't exist. One American black admitted that he moved to the West Indies and married there because he knew that never again would he want to return to a country in which he would be seen first for his color and only later for what *he himself* was.

Cassie, for instance, was the "leftover" offspring of an unsuccessful first marriage. After her father abandoned them when Cassie was twelve, her attractive and ambitious, middle-class, midwestern American mother quickly remarried and had three children by her second husband.

Cassie was in the way of this new family unit. As a teenager, she was not particularly attractive: too tall and too thin, by turns moody and quarrelsome, unsure of herself with her peers, unhappy with her family and unsuccessful in her schoolwork. Eventually she dropped out of school and moved from her small town in Wisconsin to Chicago, where she worked as a waitress in a restaurant chain. She lived alone and made few friends, and those she had were mostly people who shared her work shift.

There are some, of course, who are truly social misfits, losers or fringe people who belong to groups which are marginal in their own countries, but many are like Cassie. She felt cast out of her own family and peer group and, needing acceptance and love, reached out to whoever offered it. In Cassie's case, it was Jaime. On the first night he walked into her restaurant, she fell in love immediately with this dark-haired, handsome boy with the carefree, confident ways and gallant manners typical of his upbringing as the first son of a wealthy Latin American family.

Rebels

Jaime, on the other hand, fit into the rebel category. Beneath his suave, easy-going manner was a young man who was disenchanted with his own country, with its politics, its social mores and way of life. Since he had begun his studies at the University of Chicago, he had decided that he really never wanted to live in his own country again.

In Cassie he found a girl who personified freedom from all the things he objected to. She was someone his parents would obviously disapprove of: on the wild side, living alone, working at a menial job. She was free, and fun, and broke all the rules "nice" girls in his own country wouldn't dare break, at least not openly. And she adored him—not a small matter for a lonesome student far from his homeland.

Even so, he might not have made the break with his own culture; he might have had his fling and then returned home once his studies were completed, if Cassie had not become pregnant. Suddenly a decision was upon him. Although Cassie said she did not want him to feel obligated to marry her and refused to talk of marriage, he felt responsible to this lonely girl who was going to bear his child.

Despite his family's outrage and despite the fact that they cut off his allowance, forcing him to drop out of school (thus losing his student status and later his permission to remain in the States), he chose to turn his back on his own culture and remain with Cassie. He became a true rebel, half by choice, half by circumstance, living on the edge of society, constantly in fear of being deported.

The rebels, for one reason or another, are people who consciously or unconsciously marry cross-culturally as a form of protest against something in their own cultures which they don't like and/or want to get away from. Sometimes these are basic values or beliefs, sometimes minor or indefinable subtle dissatisfactions.

Some are like Helga, a German left-wing student radical, who was involved with an underground organization and who paired up with a Libyan she met during some of their activities and followed him back to his own country with a dream of working against injustice and towards the overthrow of capitalist systems.

Others are idealists like Bill, who, after a stint in the Peace Corps, became a lawyer dedicated to human rights. To most of his friends it seemed in character that he should marry someone from a different country, a different race. Mary, the Nigerian feminist he met at the University of California at Berkeley, was a logical choice, a perfect helpmate in the causes to which he had dedicated his life.

Lynn, a suburban New York WASP debutante, on the other hand, was merely bored with the limitations of upper-class bourgeois living. In part she was attracted to Hans, the Austrian ski instructor she met on her junior year abroad, because of his blatant disregard for all the "niceties" which had been instilled in her since birth, and in part because she saw a way to avoid being swallowed up into the lifestyle of her parents: the country club, the Episcopalian-Junior League trap of her own world.

Some of the rebels cross class as well as culture in their marriages; others cross color, religious, educational or generational lines—sometimes impulsively, sometimes intentionally.

While most young people rebel in their youth in one form or another and then return to the fold as they age, these matrimonial rebels have made a lifelong commitment to their statements of protest.

Mavericks

Another type of person who marries interculturally is the nonconformist, or the maverick. The people in this group are independents who, while belonging to and being accepted by (and not actively protesting against) their own societies, simply don't put much importance on belonging to the "in group." Frequently, but not always, they are loners—by choice. Unlike the outcasts, they are not social rejects, but people who feel detached enough from their own cultures or peer groups to want to decide for themselves the course of their lives. Often they are actually happier outside their own societies because they feel freed from pressures to join and to conform to values they don't fully share.

Zoahar, a nonmilitant Israeli, for example, felt happier with his Brazilian carioca bride, a woman he met while he was a deep-sea diving instructor at the Club Mediterranee in Martinique, than he was with the girls he met in the kibbutz. She neither knew nor cared much about what was going on in the Middle East, and living with her made him feel free of that world.

Unlike the idealist/rebels of the second group, these nonconformists often have no deep beliefs to cling to and/or don't feel tied to any social, religious or cultural groups.

Frequently, they have gone away to school at an early age and have been separated from their families and their neighborhoods; or they have moved often and have few roots which tie them to a particular place or lifestyle.

Massimo, for example, was the son of an Italian diplomat, who spent most of his life growing up in different parts of the world and knew his native Italy only slightly, as a visitor, when his parents had home leave or were posted there briefly. He spoke Spanish and English better than Italian and was fluent in French, since he had attended French schools at all their postings. He felt he was multicultural and when he met Tove, who was half-Egyptian and half-Danish, it was as much the similarity of their backgrounds and attitudes towards others which appealed to him as it was her exotic beauty.

Both felt they were free spirits and had little patience with—indeed were somewhat arrogant about—what they considered the narrow-mindedness of most of their contemporaries. When they married, they created their own lifestyle, choosing bits and pieces of the things they liked best about the many cultures they had known; they raised their children without any formal religion or obligatory social mores. They felt that they as a family were world citizens, people without the dictates, the limits, the prejudices of monocultural people. They were determined not to be confined by any one culture or forced to live in any one place. In fact, Massimo's decision to follow in his father's footsteps and become a member of the diplomatic corps permitted them to continue the "gypsy" existence he had always known.

Compensators

Compensators are people who are looking for their "better half." They are people who feel incomplete and look for someone to fill the void—real or imagined. They marry out of need; they choose someone they believe will provide them with what they covet or believe they lack.

This is not a characteristic which is exclusive to intercultural spouses. It could be said about many monocultural people too. The difference is that the intercultural compensators believe they can find what they need (or think they need) only with a foreigner. They attribute their deficiencies to their culture (their ethnic makeup, the lifestyle of their society, etc.).

Cassie, for example, was as much a compensator as she was an outcast; like most people she was a mixture of types. In part she was attracted to Jaime because of his sunny personality (in contrast to her moody one), to his smooth self-confidence (in contrast to her shyness), and in part because he had a tradition of strong family ties which she felt would make up for her own unstable family relationship. She longed to make his family her own and begged him to make peace with them.

Many compensators come from families in which there has not been a truly loving, intimate relationship among its members. Often they are from families where one or both parents are absent (either physically or emotionally) and have not had their emotional needs met as children or perhaps have never seen a healthy marital partnership function. Not knowing what to look for, they fall in love with romance. They often choose foreigners who have different ideas on how to express love or who are indifferent to their need for love but "make up" for (or disguise) the fact with their exotic ways.

Cecil, a product of nannies and British boarding schools, barely knew his parents and had little home life as a child; he was as much attracted to his Japanese wife Ikumi for her strong cohesive family as for her delicate, deferential mannerisms. Only after they were married did he realize that she was attracted by the very opposite in him (his independence). She was seeking freedom from her strong, but (to her) domineering and intrusive family. She was looking for a world in which she could put *herself* first and a man who would not make demands on her. She thought she had found this in Cecil.

Rashida never thought of herself as a compensator, and yet her life had been one long search for identity. Rashida was the privileged, only child of wealthy, Washington, D.C., black parents, who were more involved in their own social lives than in her, but tried to make up for it by giving her entreé into the white world. For most of her life she had been the only black child in white neighborhoods, the only black student in private white schools, a token black in the elite women's college she attended. When she won a national singing competition, they sent her to study voice in Rome, where she was accepted by the foreign colony and was avidly courted by Italian men, who were as intrigued by her color as her foreignness.

For most of her life she had had white friends and dated white boys, but she was never quite one of them; yet she did not feel herself to be quite black, certainly not like most of the blacks she knew. She was almost reconciled to this "Oreo" identity, as she described it—black on the outside, white on the inside— and had decided that perhaps she would remain in Rome.

Then she met Olu and was immediately attracted to this fellow black foreigner with a British accent. He had a black African background which she coveted and wanted to become a part of. When he asked her to return to Kenya with him, she knew she wanted to go. She wanted to be a black woman in a black world; she wanted the identity she had always felt was missing, the identity he could give her. With him she could recapture her roots.

None of the compensators had particularly negative feelings about their own cultures, as did the rebels, but were searching for something which they felt was missing in themselves, something they believed a foreign spouse would be able to provide.

Adventurers

In one way this group embraces all the others, for there is a little of the adventurer in all those who marry interculturally. Intercultural spouses dare to be different, to veer from the norm, to cross cultural boundaries, to abandon their home shores (figuratively or physically) and risk a lifetime on an unknown one.

But as a group, what distinguishes adventurers from the others is that they *need* the foreign touch to provide excitement in their lives. It is almost imperative. They are often bored with the comfortable, predictable relationships they have had with people of their own kind. With someone from another culture they find the sparks, the chemistry which makes life stimulating and which makes them feel special.

Hans, who had been continually exposed to foreigners in the international ski resort of St. Anton, found the women of his own culture limited and uninteresting. He dreamed of going to the United States and of taking a job as ski instructor at Copper Mountain or Aspen. He yearned to escape the humdrum routine of his mountain village. When he met Lynn, she was everything he thought he wanted: attractive, wealthy, educated, foreign, and most of all, different from women at home. Conquering her was a feather in his cap, and it gave him the prestige of a quasi-foreigner himself.

Some adventurers cross *all* boundaries—class, race, religion, age—when they marry internationally because, to them, each additional difference makes the challenge just that much more exciting. Some of them marry on impulse, for the shock effect, like Jeanpierre, the wild son of a high-ranking French diplomat who rocked the foundations of the embassy when he married the family's Ethiopian maid; or Esmeralda, the pampered daughter of a Spanish industrialist, who married a Brazilian soccer player she met during Carnival in Rio.

Escapists

The escapists are people who marry to improve the quality of their lives or to escape life in their own countries. Some are social climbers, who marry to improve their social or economic positions (which they could not do in their own countries). Others seek to escape into what they believe will be a better world—away from a desperate life, as many war brides have done. Some marry to gain citizenship in a certain country and avoid being deported. Others make trade-offs: aristocratic Old World titles in exchange for New World fortunes (or vice versa).

Indeed, most marriages of escapists are trade-offs of one kind or another. Sometimes they are straightforward business arrangements. Usually they last as long as the objectives of both are met. Anne, Jeanpierre's wife, stayed with him until he took her to Paris, where she got a job as a model, received her French citizenship, and could manage on her own. Esmeralda's husband bent to her every wish until he was well established in the jet-set society he had envied for so long.

Unstables

While most intercultural marriages are between normal people, there are those who marry for sadistic, masochistic or neurotic reasons.[4]

In some cultures, anyone who veers from the norm by marrying someone different from themselves is considered abnormal and sometimes even deviant by their societies; and in some religions, marriage with someone of another faith is forbidden for these reasons.

Any one of the previous types we've described in an *extreme* form might fall under the unstable category.

Jeanpierre is one example. His marriage to Anne was as much a reaction against his demanding, perfectionist father and rigid, snobbish mother as it was a statement of his own poor self-esteem. He was unable to deal with the anxiety and emotional intensity his relationship with his parents produced, and he attempted to escape by marrying an unsuitable foreigner. In a confused way, however, he also set about finding the person who would enable him to duplicate the emotional environment he had experienced in his own home.

He mistreated Ann, believing she would stay with him, no matter what, out of gratitude for the kind of life he was able to

---

[4] For further discussion of this topic, see "Motivations for Intercultural Marriage," by Walter F. Char in *Adjustment in Intercultural Marriage,* p. 39.

give her. He was shocked years later when she left him, but he attributed her desertion to her "cultural inferiority" rather than to his own behavior.

While proportionately there are not many of these kinds of unstable marriages (as defined here), they do exist, and many survive. As long as the motives which bound the couple together in the first place continue to function and as long as each one (or at least the dominant partner) is getting what he/she wants from the relationship, the marriage will endure.[5]

We have not given much space to love in our discussion of marital motives, although most of the couples involved cited love as their primary motive. Certainly in one form or another, it played a part, but *love* is defined differently by different cultures—something which many intercultural spouses have learned to their dismay only after they are married.

In many cultures romantic love is not considered a valid or necessary motive for marriage. It is associated with *eros* or passion and is felt to have no important part in forming a new family. However, when similar goals and values in life transcend cultural barriers, love can indeed be considered a principal motive for marriage.

PHASES OF ADJUSTMENT

Now we are going to consider what happens as each partner sheds the accoutrements of single life and builds a "new, private sphere which is the special turf of the two people involved... [as each one decides] what the themes of their new, jointly constructed scenario will be."[6]

If you have been married for a while, try to recall various phases of your relationship—how and when certain attitudes and behavior patterns developed. You will be able to pinpoint some things exactly; others probably came about so subtly it will be difficult to recall their absence.

[5] Ibid, pp 33-40.
[6] Maggie Scarf, *Intimate Partners*, p 35.

There are several phases in marital relationships and, while acknowledging that the form and the details vary with each couple and set of circumstances, we are going to describe them under three general headings:

1.   The Honeymoon Phase, when everything new is a wonderful, enriching gift

2.   The Settling-in Phase, when some of the differences become issues

3.   The Resolution, when the differences are either resolved or accepted, or the conflicts become habits.

Phase 1: Honeymoon

Some couples know each other well when they marry and also know a great deal about each other's cultures. As a result they are fairly well prepared for what their joint future holds. Others have married more impulsively and without much preparation. Nonetheless, most intercultural couples go through all three phases before they work out "whose ideas about reality will be the stronger ones."[7]

The honeymoon phase is a period in which everything new is exciting, and the differences which appear are seen as romantic and attractive. The mood of the partners is one of optimism and confidence. They feel exhilarated and approach their marriage with the enthusiasm of two people who are concocting a wonderful international cocktail, using all the best ingredients of their two worlds: the different traditions, customs, folklore, art, holidays, myths, food, language, music, friends.

Lynn and Hans described their early days as being like "a giant slalom" into which they put all their efforts and energies to make the most of the new territory into which they were catapulting. Cassie and Jaime said they felt as though they were

---

[7] *Ibid,* p 36.

"playing house with musical chairs." It was confusing, dizzying, a bit "heady and crazy, but fun."

For some couples this phase lasts quite a while, ending only with the intrusion of some outside circumstance or some problem which causes strain on both of them. But most couples move quite rapidly into phase 2, when many of the differences which attracted them to each other in the first place are seen as obstacles to the fulfillment of each one's particular expectations. The couple begins to see what really *is* different and to realize what the differences mean for their lives together.

Phase 2: Settling-in

As the novelty of the marriage wears off, and some of the politeness and good behavior between the spouses is shed, the partners begin to fall back into old habits and manners and expose sides of themselves, both personal and cultural, which, while not necessarily hidden, were not obvious before. It is the period in which both spouses begin defending their own right ways against foreign assault and when their differing notions about life and marriage surface.

When the ski season ended, the honeymoon was over for debutante Lynn and her Austrian husband, Hans. Lynn remembers feeling the first shadows of discontent, which she attributed to the gloomy weather and slow pace of life. There was no doubt in her mind that she still loved her handsome husband (though he didn't look quite as dashing out of his ski instructor's jumpsuit and sunglasses, and he didn't bathe quite as often as she would have liked).

The beauties of the landscape surrounding St. Anton still awed her, but their tiny apartment seemed to have walls that closed in on her as the snow turned to rain and the streets outside to slush. As the hotels and restaurants shut down one by one and the tourists departed, Hans took to spending long hours with his fellow instructors, drinking in the corner coffeehouse to while away the time until the summer mountain climbing season began.

Lynn found she didn't have enough books in English to read; she missed having a real girlfriend she could talk to—the women there seemed different. There was no one she could confide in or do things with.

She sensed that Hans might be having second thoughts about their impulsive marriage. He seemed to be fussing at her all the time, trying to transform her into a typical hausfrau—something he had always said he didn't want. He had claimed that he chose to marry her *because* she was different.

Hans, in turn, who had automatically returned to his old routines, bristled under Lynn's complaints about the time he spent away from her with his friends. He became conscious of the fact that she didn't know how to run a house or cook more than hamburgers, that she always had her nose in a book (in English to boot), that she didn't make friends with other women, and that she complained about being alone and about the heating in the apartment instead of dressing properly. They collected little gripes about one another, which began to strain their tolerance, tarnishing the glow of their relationship.

Cassie and Jaime seemed to suit each other well until Jennifer was born. Then Cassie had to quit work and stay home to care for the baby; there were no grandparents or relatives to help out. Jaime had to find a job to support his new family, something which was easier said than done without proper papers or fluency in English. He knew he would have his papers eventually, the green card which would permit him to stay in the country,[8] but that took time and they needed money now!

At first he was disbelieving, then frustrated and angry as he was turned down at place after place, despite his years of college and his privileged background. Finally he found a job as a short-order cook in Cassie's old restaurant, at a salary which was less than he had previously received as an allowance from his parents for himself alone.

Jaime was demoralized at having to perform manual labor; his masculinity offended. Overnight he seemed to change from

---

[8] Although he and Cassie were not married, as Jennifer's father he was entitled by law to legal status.

a carefree, lighthearted boy to a demanding, impatient despot. He began asserting his authority at home in "funny little ways," according to Cassie—to become the man at home he was prevented from being in the outside world.

He berated Cassie for her irresponsible ways and criticized her friends, complaining that she saw too much of them. He wanted her home, alone, with the baby, being a mother. He wanted her to cook his national dishes, to learn his language, and to dress like a señora.

Both of these couples were deep into phase 2 before they knew what was happening. Suddenly they became aware that not only were their personalities different, but their culturally-based ideas about life and correct behavior contrasted also.

In phase 2 cultural variants are no longer simply different accents or physical characteristics, but basic realities which are expressed in questions such as: "Why shouldn't a woman go out alone?" "Who is changing the diapers?" "Do you people always yell when you talk?" "Must we always have a brother/cousin/friend living with us?" The differences become perplexing, some of them alarming and others merely irritants.

When couples begin to hew out a routine for their lives they become more aware of the differences than of the similarities between them. They actually see more differences than similarities. The differences seem more negative than positive, and the negative differences appear bigger, more ominous, even overwhelming.

Love begins taking a back seat to compatibility. The old saying states that similarity leads to compatibility, dissimilarity to incompatibility. The more differences there are and the more severe, the more difficult it is for a couple to live compatibly.

Of course, this is not always true. Some differences are complementary; they are good for harmony and balance. A moody person may benefit from association with a carefree one, and an explosive personality may need a calm, cool partner to keep matters in control. Some differences, while not complementary, are compatible in that they don't conflict with or obstruct the other: the artist and the scientist may have dissimilar interests, but they are not mutually exclusive.

Other differences, unfortunately, increase disharmony, especially when they are numerous or extreme or when the marriage is already under strain for other reasons. Then, differences can become intolerable.

When the strain reaches crisis point in an intercultural marriage, the couple generally focuses on the cultural differences, often exaggerating them and blaming them for every problem.

Why is this? One reason is that cultural differences are easy to spot. People often don't know what they are fighting about and reach out to find something obvious. Sometimes the real reasons for the strained marriages are too deep to be seen clearly or too sensitive for the couple to face, and cultural diversities are easy targets.

Cassie's ways were different from those of Jaime's mother and sister (who were his closest examples of what real women should be), and so he attacked her ways as being unfeminine. He blamed Cassie for his angry flare-ups, instead of facing what was really bothering him: his fears and frustrations as a new father, principal wage earner, and an illegal alien. Her "American feminist" behavior was different from his culturally-bred expectations and thus became a scapegoat for his true problems.

In some cases, people have simply married the wrong *partner*, not the wrong culture, and can't accept or understand that cultural differences have little or nothing to do with their real problems. When they run into the first snags in the relationship, instead of admitting they might have made the wrong choice, they make culture the culprit.

Anne and Jeanpierre, who had no valid basis for their marriage, cited, respectively, both "French egotism" and "Ethiopian backwardness" for the failure of their marriage. They talked in stereotypes. Both refused to face up to their own personal deficiencies which, combined with their cultural differences, made their union an impossible one from the very start.

There is no doubt that intercultural marriages take more effort than other marriages because there are so many more elements to be blended. Some people are simply not prepared to make that extra effort. They are mired in their ethnocentric positions, refusing to budge from comfortable viewpoints (which they often call principles) and then use the differences in cultures as an excuse. They fall back on stereotypes: "He is just too Chinese/Greek/German to understand." "It's no use." "I'm an Italian/American/Senegalese and we don't/do put up with this/ that," and so on. Anything different is wrong or inferior and, therefore, the cause of the problems.

It is incorrect, however, to say that cultural differences don't count because there are some which do indeed jeopardize marital compatibility and threaten marital success. This holds true, especially, for the differences which have to do with ways of relating (showing love and caring), communicating, and reacting to stressful events.[9]

Milee, a Vietnamese war bride, spoke of wrapping herself into a silent knot in reaction to the fear and loneliness she experienced upon arriving in her new country. She felt insecure and abandoned by her gregarious Australian husband, Harry, who in turn misread her behavior as antisocial, and antagonistic towards his friends and homeland.

Instead of responding to her unspoken cry for reassurance and companionship, he reacted by staying out more and more with his drinking buddies who Milee then did come to resent as intruders who were taking her husband away from her. This cycle of hurt, accusations, and resentment continued to build. Neither one of them knew what to do.

Harry didn't understand that she couldn't express to him verbally her inner feelings, that she expected him to be able to intuit them if he loved her; and Milee didn't understand that he was escaping from what he saw as her silent hostility towards him. Only when they found help from a third party, who was

[9] Stressful events can be defined as those events that push us beyond a normal, neutral state—events such as a death, a birth, moves, and changes in status and/or style of living. Stress is the response of the body to the demands on it for adaptation or adjustment to the event.

familiar with both cultures, were they able to unravel the skein of misunderstandings.

Problems of this kind often involve multiple aspects. On one front it is a question of *communication*. People often don't understand each other's messages because they have different ways of sending and receiving them (a problem common to all marriages but complicated by the culturally different ways of expressing emotion). On another front it is the degree to which each has a *sensitivity* to and appreciation for the other's different needs—needs which are possibly not shared. Emotional responses to stressful situations may be not only culturally different, but culturally conflicting as well.

Although British Cecil learned to understand that his freedom-seeking Japanese wife giggled when she was upset or frightened, he could not relate to it, just as Ikumi couldn't reconcile herself to the fact that when Cecil was upset, he reacted in anger. Each resented the other's ways and responded inappropriately. Understanding was not enough; both had to learn to allow for the other's differentness instead of reacting to each other from their own cultural viewpoints.

When intercultural couples are well into the settling-in phase, some (or many) of their differences may crop up again and again as troublespots in the effort to find the right fit for their different personalities and different cultures. These troublespots are the focus of part two.

Phase 3: Resolution

What happens at this point in the marriage depends entirely on the particular couple. Some resolve their difficulties by habitually fighting them out, usually from their original starting points, and continue doing so, time after time, until the end of their marriages (or of their lives). As one American-Japanese couple put it: "I rant and rave and screech and he gives me the silent treatment. When we get tired of it all, we make love and that's that. Nothing's solved, but it no longer seems that important...until the next time it comes up." They never really resolve anything; they simply streamline their fighting methods. This then becomes "their way" of handling their differences.

Others turn their backs on the issues. They try to ignore them and pretend they don't even exist. Neither partner is converted to the other's point of view and, knowing that discussion about the problem will always end up in a fight, choose to banish or ignore it. Some choose to live separate though loosely connected lives. The issue of their separateness seethes beneath their relationship but is never permitted to explode. Many consider this a resolution because they are convinced that there is no other answer for them.

As we will see in part 3, there is another way to manage the issues: one in which each partner allows for the other's differentness without giving up his or her own. These couples have found ways to identify and separate the real issues from the red herrings and then get to work confronting and resolving the ones that count.

FOOD,
FRIENDS,
AND OTHER
FRUSTRATIONS

PART 2

POTENTIAL PITFALLS

Not all differences cause problems for intercultural couples and even those which easily can and often do, don't cause problems for everyone. Making a definitive list of potential troublespots is a problem. Not only is the personality mixture different for each couple (as it is in all marriages), but in intercultural marriages there are inexhaustible possibilities for unique mixtures of cultural values, assumptions and beliefs, religions, races, educational and social backgrounds, etc.

However, there are enough areas which are continually cited as troublespots by intercultural couples to make it possible to draw up a list of potential pitfalls. Obviously, those reading this book will have their own list of intercultural challenges, some of which will match the ones listed here. But almost all the couples interviewed for this book agreed that the areas listed below could become problems for the intercultural couple.

It must be kept in mind that we are merely presenting the issues in part two, whereas in part three we will offer some practical solutions. However, bear in mind that while many of the issues are shared by most of the couples, the resolution of each is a purely personal matter, depending on the makeup of each individual couple.

Here is our list of potential troublespots for intercultural marriages.

1. Values	10. In-laws
2. Food and Drink	11. Social Class
3. Sex	12. Religion
4. Male-Female Roles	13. Raising Children
5. Time	14. Language/Communication
6. Place of Residence	15. Dealing with Stress
7. Politics	16. Illness and Suffering
8. Friends	17. Ethnocentrism
9. Finances	

Some issues appear to overlap (sex and male-female roles, for example, or religion and values), but there are important distinctions between them, and they merit separate discussion.

We have also listed areas which may seem trivial, such as food or time, but married life is made up of day-to-day trivia, and underlying the apparent trivia, there are deeply rooted personal or cultural values.

Most of these areas are potentially problematic to all marriages, not just to intercultural ones. However, it is the degree to which they exist which is not the same. In intercultural marriages the differences are often extreme, involving cultural identity, and thereby are unconscious and more difficult to resolve. And, the more different the cultures, the more difficult the job.

Some couples insist that cultural differences are not issues at all (if two people are truly in love... etc., etc.). This does not mean they are not issues. It usually means that these couples don't see the differences as cultural issues or that they have somehow managed to overcome or resolve them without being aware of what they were doing, or, that in their particular personal/cultural mix, certain differences were unimportant. But generally speaking, differences do indeed exist and are challenges for the intercultural couple.

Let's look at the issues, one by one, and see how they often become problems.

Values

Man is the only animal that laughs and weeps: for he is the only animal that is struck with the difference between what things are and what they ought to be.
—William Hazlitt, *Table Talk*

We begin our discussion with values because they are central to virtually everything because that which means enough to become an issue in an intercultural marriage is based on a value, whether knowingly or unknowingly, intentionally or unintentionally.

The word *value* comes from the Latin *valere*, which means "to be worth." In fact, as we use the term, *values* indicates what matters, what is seen as good and bad, right and wrong, true and false, important and unimportant. Values tell us much about who we are, what we believe in, and how we will evaluate behavior.

Values are taught in the home, often unconsciously, and reinforced by society; so we can say that values are generally culturally determined.

The ancient Greek philosophers, Aristotle and Plato, said that human beings desire real goods and apparent goods. Simplistically put, real goods are things we *need;* apparent goods are things we *want*. Needs are inherent or natural (we are born with them) and universal, but often unconscious. Wants are acquired (bred into us by environment, circumstances), individual, and conscious (we know what we want).

People of different cultures, while having the same fundamental needs, may very well have not only quite different wants, but quite different ways of perceiving their needs. This difference in perception can present an almost insurmountable obstacle for an intercultural couple. It is further complicated by the fact that many, if not most, of their behavior patterns are based on unconscious values and cultural assumptions about how life should best be lived.

Well-known psychologist Edward Stewart in his book *American Cultural Patterns: A Cross-Cultural Perspective*, offers a model[10] for better understanding the nature of these assumptions and values and how they vary from culture to culture.

Stewart divides cultural values and assumptions into four components which he then analyzes from a cross-cultural perspective: (1) form of activity, (2) form of relation to others, (3) perception of the world, (4) perception of self. Here are examples of the kind of things which fall under each component.

Under "form of activity" Stewart compares the North American orientation towards "doing" (working as an active way of forming the future; making and being responsible for one's own decisions, etc.) with the orientation of other cultures in which "being" is the more predominant value (living for and making the most of, or enjoying the present), and with still others which are oriented towards "being-in-becoming" (or self-growth).

Under "form of relation to others" he compares the North American orientation towards equality (treating all people the same) and easily established but relatively impermanent relationships with the status conscious, formal, longer lasting, and involved relationships common to many other cultures.

Under "perception of the world" he compares the ways different cultures consider humankind's relation to nature (North Americans see humans as separate from nature, while many other cultures see humans as an integral part of it) and shows how they deal with the world around them (exploiting it for their own needs vs. respecting or fearing it as a force of some sort beyond human control).

And finally, under "perception of self" he compares the ways people in different societies conceive of themselves (as separate individuals or as part of a tightly-knit group) and how

[10] Edward C. Stewart, *American Cultural Patterns*, p 31.

that affects the way they behave (emphasizing a reliance on self-motivation or acting in terms of obligation toward a group).[11]

For the intercultural couple this means that there may be complex differences in values behind many of the issues causing trouble in their marriage—made all the more complex because those values are obscure. Most spouses don't know much about their own cultural value orientation, much less that of their partner's. They just know that "something" isn't working right.

Dorrie, a Dutch-English woman who married a Japanese man she met in graduate school in the U.S. (she was the student, he the exalted professor), explained that it took her many years to begin to "spot the value differences which were at the bottom of most of our fights."

A seemingly trivial example explained what she meant. Like most Japanese, Dorrie and her husband Hiroshi slept on *futon*, Japanese-style mattress pad and quilts, which are hung out to air as often as possible. As Dorrie and Hiroshi lived in an apartment, that meant hanging them over the balcony which she always did "with the side we sleep on facing out to get the most air and sun." Hiroshi regularly berated her for not hanging them so that the "pretty side" was out for others to see. He placed emphasis on appearance and was concerned about the impression they would make on neighbors while she was more concerned about how much fresh air and sunlight the used side of the bedding would get. Behind this were two sets of cultural values which in this case happened to conflict.

This is a minor example of how value differences cause disagreement or misunderstanding. In dealing with major issues, these differences can cause massive upsets in couple compatibility. Frequently the couples never learn to identify what is behind the conflict.

While culture affects most people deeply, not everyone adheres to the dominant values of his or her culture. Within each group are subgroups which may actually oppose the

---

[11] Stewart based his analysis on the "Kluckhohn Model," developed by Kluckhohn and Strodtbeck in *Variations in Value Orientations,* chapter 1.

mainstream values. You will find intercultural couples whose personal values do not coincide with the predominant cultural values of their society and who often identify more with those of the culture of the spouse. Generally, people who enter into an intercultural marriage have already distanced themselves somewhat from a strict adherence to the predominant values of their own societies. But, at the same time, they are what they are because of their society's value orientation. Whether they personally believe in those values or not, they were shaped by a society which espoused them.

For example, although Jaime was a rebel who turned his back on his culture, he was still a product of its values. He wanted to be free, like a North American, to marry the girl of his choice, but his response to the menial job his choice forced him to accept was typically Latin American. He was outraged at the loss of dignity. Serving those he considered to be his inferiors clashed with his view of the way things were *supposed* to be; his background and social class demanded more. He was losing face, something which mattered to him, and he resented it.

Cassie, on the other hand, saw his job as a temporary expedient. To her it was a means to an end, and she couldn't understand why he was making such a big fuss about it.

Deirdre is another individual who sought to find, in her partner's culture, the values which she personally espoused but which did not coincide with the dominant values of her society. Deirdre was an Irish woman who at an early age had emigrated to the United States and had been raised by energetic Irish Catholic relatives. She was more of a "be-er" than a "doer" and felt out of step with the society around her. She was more at home with people who attended to intellectual pursuits and spiritual growth than with those who were seeking business success. She seemed to get along with Latins and Hispanics who, she felt, were more interested in the life of the mind and knew how to have a better time than their Anglo-Saxon counterparts. When she met Mario, she was so taken in by his playboy charm that she didn't see the man beneath who, in other ways, was atypical of his own culture, and much more concerned with achievement and empire building than in spiritual growth. Ironically, this is not an unusual occurrence in intercultural marriage—each partner in some important respect may identify more with the culture of the person they married than with their own.

At the other end of the spectrum are couples from cultures so widely divergent in the way right and wrong and good and bad are perceived that it is impossible for those who strictly adhere to their cultural tenets to coexist peaceably under the same roof. The key word here is *strictly.*

Yvette and Ali, the French-Kuwaiti couple we met at the beginning of the book, were about as culturally different as two people could be. There was no way that Yvette, a baptized (although not church-going) Catholic, could share many of Ali's values as dictated by his Islamic religion. Fortunately for them as a couple, Ali personally believed that each person should interpret the word of Allah in his own way and live accordingly, and he defended his wife against criticism from more stringent Muslims. But this tolerance, and the understanding based on it, had to be continually worked at in their daily lives, especially when they had children who had to be taught right from wrong and true from false.

Marriages between people with conflicting values can work, but there must be more similarities in values than there are differences. Where there are conflicting values, the couple has to find a solution, and to do this, they each have to be ready to give a little.[12]

When the couple's conflicting values are deeply ingrained and unconscious or where one or both of the partners is inflexible (will not admit to the existence of another value system), the marriage will be threatened. For it is only by understanding and being able to allow for one another's uniqueness, even regarding deeply held convictions about how life should be lived, that a married couple can continue to live in harmony.

[12] For more on this, see Condon and Yousef's "Something of Values," *An Introduction to Intercultural Communication*, pp 47-62.

Food and Drink

What is food to one is another's bitter poison.
—Lucretius, *On the Nature of Things*

In nearly all cultures food is used to celebrate life events—to mark births, deaths, weddings, rites of passage; to celebrate and to console. It is the main part of many ceremonies and rituals, both lay and religious, but it is also a mainstay of daily life. It is what keeps body and soul together and, as such, can be one of the most sticky of the cultural issues.

Cookbooks from around the world show the diversities of taste and methods of preparing food; etiquette books point out different ideas of good and bad manners and culinary protocol. Food brings out the characteristics of a people in many other ways: it shows something of the male-female relationship and roles, of the importance of family and religion, and of the lifestyle and values of a people.

Arabs enforce family unity around the dinner table; the Irish drink at wakes;[13] the Japanese express Zen aesthetics through ritual tea ceremonies; and the Jewish son shows love for his mother in proportion to his appetite. In Italy a woman's femininity has traditionally been judged according to how much time she spends bending over the stove or kneading dough for the pasta. In certain Middle Eastern and African countries, the men eat alone and the women cook (or supervise the cooking) and serve. In others, where the women must not go out alone, the husband buys the food and the wife prepares the meal with what he chooses. In Tunisia mealtimes are flexible and punctuality not important; therefore, the foods are such that they can be prepared ahead and reheated. In North America frozen dinners are popped into the oven or microwave, freeing the cook and demonstrating the fast-paced, fragmented lifestyle of Americans.

[13] In Anglo-Irish families food is almost always less important than drink as a tool of celebration (and their lack of culinary prowess is an indication of the secondary importance people place on food).

Vive la différence!—until people from different cultural backgrounds are living in the same house and dealing with differences three times a day. In fact no other single difference was cited as often by couples as a problem than food. Its significance goes far beyond the digestive tract. The intercultural couple has to work out house rules which satisfy them both, not only in terms of what is served, but also how it is served (and by whom), who cooks, and who cleans up. These seemingly minor issues become bones of contention between the spouses, precisely because they contain so many underlying meanings and spring from so many unconscious sources.

Basically we can say that the food issue includes the following categories:

1. What is eaten (and drunk) and how it is prepared

2. When the main meal is served—at noon or at nine

3. Where the meal is eaten: in public or in private, in the car, on the street, in the kitchen on the run, or with the *pater familias* at the head of a formal dinner table

4. How it is eaten (manners, utensils, etc.)

What Is Eaten

Fish and chips...sushi...fejoiada...matouke...peanut butter...curry...lasagne...wonton...blood sausage...stuffed vine leaves...and so on. The list is endless, and each food is a mainstay to someone.

Religious taboos and special customs enter in: Muslim law prohibits the consumption of alcoholic beverages, pork and shellfish; Hindus and Buddhists avoid beef; Catholics fast on Good Friday; Jews observe Passover.

Some people are open to experimentation while others are tied psychologically to certain tastes. Others may not be able to digest the ethnic fare of the partner or may be allergic to it.

One Swedish husband, Sune, complained that the smell of his wife Rani's Malaysian cooking nauseated him.[14] Victor, who was used to homogenized Swiss fare, had to swallow his horror (and more) when his Tunisian mother-in-law "honored" him with the choice morsel at their first dinner together: the bubbling eye which stared out at him from the skewered sheep's head roasting over the hearth.

More often the couple's food problems are subtle ones, based on what each one is used to and prefers in his/her home: a meal is not a meal without borscht, without rice, without fresh bread, without meat and potatoes, and so on.

Longing for one's own foods may play a powerful psychological role, especially in the lives of the spouses who have left their homelands to live in their partner's country. The American may wish for a hamburger and milkshake to soothe a bout of homesickness; the British, for a traditional pudding at Christmas; the Vietnamese, for a meal of rice and ginger chicken shared with friends and relatives.

Occasionally, the disdain one partner feels for the food (or manner of preparing or eating) of the other becomes a silent reproach of something essential to the other.

There is an old adage: "The way to a man's heart is through his stomach," and usually the stomach wants the kind of food it is used to. Love is shown in a lot of ways, but in many cultures love is judged by the time and care put into preparing the repast. In others, food preparation is much less significant as an indicator of love and devotion. What does matter is that the spouses know how important food and its preparation are to the other and reach a compromise.

Yvette, who had met her Kuwaiti husband when both were students in England, resented it when he called her from her studies to bring him a cup of tea, something he could easily have done for himself. He was puzzled by her view of this simple ritual

---

[14] Almost everyone tends to prefer the smells one grew up with and which ring the bells of childhood memories; some never accept alien aromas.

as a sexist demand. Later she learned to accept such requests as his way of using a food ritual to call her attention to him, of asking her to demonstrate her love for him.

When the Meal Is Served

Sara, a stewardess for Air Canada, had lived alone and had her free time to herself before her marriage to Joachim, an established Portuguese industrialist. When he was working, she thought she would be free to spend her days as she chose. But he saw things differently, and their controversy over the noon meal was their earliest and most continuous battle. She maintained that she had promised "for better, for worse, but never for lunch." Joachim expected an elaborate noon feast. She found that her whole life was scheduled around this intrusive constant: shopping for lunch, preparing it, eating it, and cleaning up after it. Her days were no longer free and she became increasingly resentful. He was offended by her neglectful attitude toward her wifely role and reproached her for her inability to conform to the customs of his country, where everything shut down for three hours in the middle of the day and all married men went home for the main meal and a rest.

For many intercultural couples, mealtime is an issue. Some of them cannot accustom their stomachs to new schedules: one may simply not be hungry at noon, or the other may not be able to eat a big meal at night. Some want to eat at the same time every day while others prefer to eat when they are hungry. Much depends on the degree of formality in the family they grew up in, and this often depends on where the family is from.

Where the Meal Is Eaten

Where a family chooses to eat its main meal varies also and tells a great deal about whether the family is formal or informal, united or fragmented, authoritarian or permissive.

For Sara and Joachim, the noon meal was a problem not only in regard to what and when, but to where. Not for him was a meal to be snapped up while perched on a stool in the kitchen. It was a formal affair in which the entire family met around the table in the dining room, which was set with a tablecloth and silver and preferably was served by someone in white gloves— every day, not just on Sunday. When the children were old enough to join them, the noon meal became a time of instruction on etiquette as well: how to sit, chew, be served, and use utensils (a problem, since he and Sara held their forks in opposite hands—they finally opted for the way of his land). In the best of moments it was a time to be together, to share what was going on in their lives; in the worst (to Sara) it was a time of tempers, torture and bad digestion.

How the Meal Is Eaten

How the meal is eaten also depends on the customs and manners of each partner's culture. Sara and Joachim held their forks in different hands; Cecil used a fork and knife, and Ikumi chopsticks; Jeanpierre used monogrammed utensils and linens, and Anne had grown up with mostly finger food.

Other couples have to decide how the table is to be set (if it is to be set), who sits and who serves, and what constitutes good or bad manners according to their own family rules. In some cultures it is appropriate to slurp soup or burp to indicate appreciation of the meal, while in others such behavior would raise eyebrows.

Joachim considered it ill-mannered to eat fruit at the table with one's hands, and Sara was defeated by having to peel and slice oranges with a knife and fork. She thought paper napkins made sense with small children, but they were repugnant to Joachim.

These small things can be daily irritants; often one partner is disdainful of the other's "bad" manners. One partner may resent being pressured to conform to unfamiliar customs which may not be admired, while the other complains because the partner hasn't managed to adapt well. When there are children, the couple may argue continually about the whole matter, creating a tug-of-war at mealtime.

Sex

The war between men and women.
—James Thurber, *New Yorker* magazine

Somebody once said that in every sexual relationship, a couple takes four sets of grandparents to bed with them. What this means is that each partner is the product of sex education passed down from what the grandparents taught the parents, and each brings a version of (or reaction to) their mores, credos and expectations into his or her own marriage—whether consciously or not.

In any case, this is a startling image, and if we think of it in terms of intercultural marriages, with the vast range of possible different beliefs, behaviors and attitudes vying for position under one blanket, we see why sex can become a real issue.

Simply listing some of the things which can be viewed differently by people from different cultures gives some idea of how great the sex issue might be in these marriages:

> arranged marriage, contraception, menstruation, circumcision, masturbation, the number (and importance) of children in a family, virginity and chastity, family honor, adolescent rites, machismo and femininity, hygiene, premarital relations, marital fidelity, sexual practices, homosexuality, prostitution, incest, dating, dancing, romance, holding hands, using makeup, and "provocative" dress.

One reason sex can be a problem in intercultural marriage is that many, especially young, inexperienced people, don't expect it to be. Many people are prepared for differences in ways of eating, dressing, or talking, but they assume that sex is sex—which, of course, it is, but with infinite variety in its expression. So, perhaps out of primness or embarrassment, they don't find out beforehand about possible differences in beliefs, behaviors, and expectations, and how these will apply to their conjugal futures. They don't discuss their needs and wants and perhaps have not yet even defined them.

Couples who have lived together before marriage have some practical advantages, but they can be in for surprises also when marriage changes the format of their relationship as independent lovers and they begin to play the role (as each one sees it) of husband and wife.

Yvette, for example, commented that Ali, who had been attentive to her needs and affectionate in his lovemaking when they were living together, not only stopped being so once they were married but was actually disconcerted by her need for cuddling and kissing; he was, as he said, put off by her demands for sexual satisfaction and felt that her behavior was inappropriate for a wife, even improper.

American Rashida discovered many years after they were married that, although her Kenyan husband Olu had willingly participated in premarital sex with her, the fact that she had permitted it caused him to distrust her for the rest of their married lives. He felt that if she had slept with him, she was capable of "sinning" in that way in the future. The fact that she told him he was the only one did not pacify him, and any action of hers which he could interpret as provocative, he saw as a sign of her wantonness. To her dismay, he even considered her style of dress, use of makeup, and relationships with single friends inappropriate for a married woman.

Dutch Protestant Dorrie, on the other hand, was upset about what she called "the gymnastic, uninhibited sex" her Japanese husband preferred and which she found somewhat shocking and upsetting. "It is all so cut and dried," she commented, "technically perfect but lacking in the displays of affection I need. Where is the wine, the romance?"

Couples with the same religious background have an advantage in that they know what the moral dictates of the religion are and can agree (to some extent) on what is and is not permitted (or required) in sexual matters. But as Irish-Catholic Deirdre discovered with her wandering Italian-Catholic husband, the same religion does not always mean similar moral education because that religion is often interpreted in different ways cross-culturally. Sins may be sins, but in certain cultures they are mortal and in others venal. The difference is the degree of guilt associated with the sin. In certain male-dominant cultures, the double standard is more pronounced; what is sinful for a woman is overlooked in men.

Much depends on how differing cultures view the meaning of marriage, the role of romantic love, and the position women hold in general (and thus in the marital relationship). In marriages in which the woman is the server and the man the master, the woman's pleasure will be of little importance—certainly second to the man's.

Although Rashida and Olu's marriage was a true love story, behind this story were his beliefs that women exist to serve men, that marriage means family, and that procreation is the main purpose of sex; i.e., having children certifies the validity of the marriage. Rashida was pressured, not only by Olu, but by his entire family to begin a family immediately (with the ever present unspoken threat of his possibly taking a second wife if she didn't).

In societies where marriage is seen primarily as a romantic union of two people (most frequently egalitarian societies), the pleasure and needs of the two partners (both physical and psychological) will be important. Sex, although important, may take second place to other things; and when marriage is between equals, the sexual life of the couple will follow patterns of give-and-take and mutual pleasure-giving and seeking.

Even in cultures where romantic love is important, however, there may be quite different ways of expressing that love, i.e., how sex is used to give or deny love, how openly it is discussed, or how lustily it is enjoyed.

Many couples manage to work out their culturally-based sexual differences with few problems, especially if they happen to be of the same social and educational backgrounds, the same generation and religion, with basically the same moral values. Some couples only have problems when they become parents—when the role of mother/father is added to that of husband/wife. From the moment of pregnancy there is often a change on the part of one or the other partner in his/her attitude or treatment of the other, which is reflected in their sexual practices.

When the couple become parents, many old mores and taboos, which may have been abandoned or compromised in the enthusiasm of romance, often return to the foreground. Then the real challenge begins. For when there are children to educate, each parent reverts (often unconsciously) to what he or she was taught during childhood, so as to pass along the right moral code to the children.

Jaime, the student from Santo Domingo, who was originally attracted to Cassie because of her free ways, criticized her for those very ways when it came time to inculcate in their daughter a philosophy of life. What was all right for him and Cassie was wrong when it came to educating Jennifer.

Olu frequently threatened Rashida that he was going to take their boys from her and send them to his mother to be educated in the right way. Their sons' sexual (as well as intellectual) education was a source of constant conflict between them.

Swiss Victor was amazed when his wife, Zehyra, who he thought had become sophisticated and worldly, began imparting her Tunisian mores and customs to their adolescent daughter. He especially disagreed with her insistence that the girl shave her entire body in order to be considered clean and attractive.

Sometimes cultural differences in sexual customs and beliefs can cover up other problems in the marriage. One American man who hurriedly married an Iranian woman about to be expatriated from the States was anxious to help her overcome her sexual fears on their wedding night and coaxed her into complying with his wishes. She, however, did not want to lose her virginity because she did not plan to be married for long to this man. She knew it would be all over for her with her own countrymen if she consummated the marriage. After the honeymoon she accused her husband of rape, a charge she later used as grounds for divorce.

The free-spirited carioca, Maria Clotilde, did not want her son to undergo the formal ceremony of circumcision, (which was part of Zoahar's Israeli culture) in which guests were invited and a professional circumciser hired for the occasion. She accepted it but with some difficulty.

As is true for all the issues being considered, much depends on just how culturally different the two people are, how much importance they each give to their culture's dictates regarding sex, and how much importance they themselves attach to sex in their relationship.

Male-Female Roles

Marriage *n*. The state or condition of a community consisting of a master, a mistress and two slaves, making in all, two.
—Ambrose Bierce, *The Devil's Dictionary*

In even the most progressive societies, true equality between the sexes is more a goal than a reality. As pointed out by Condon and Yousef in their book, *An Introduction to Intercultural Communication*, it is the *form* of male superiority which differs from culture to culture.

In some societies, primarily non-Western ones, "The woman's role is to serve the man—including doing hard physical labor, deferring to his judgments and socially subordinating herself in such ways as walking behind him and eating after he has eaten."[15]

In Western societies, on the other hand, male dominance takes a more subtle form: the woman is afforded certain courtesies (which designate her as the weaker sex) and certain

---

[15] Condon and Yousef, p 70.

customs are followed which show that it is the man who has the authority. These can be seen by noting who holds the door, pays the check in the restaurant, buys the house, or takes the other's name when marrying.

"In either case there are many activities that are limited to men and others that are the exclusive province of women—but *the specific activities vary considerably from culture to culture.*"[16] (my italics)

When two people from cultures which view these activities differently marry and attempt to build a familial structure, the differences may become an issue. This is especially true if (1) the societies are culturally far apart; (2) one or both of the partners adheres strictly to his/her society's interpretation of gender roles; (3) the man comes from the more male-dominant culture and the woman from the more egalitarian one; and (4) the couple lives in the country with the stricter male-female role delineation.

If one of the partners is forced to adhere to a more severe role delineation than was customary at home, there may be problems, and the wider the gap between the partners' cultures, the more severe those problems may be.

One young woman from Iceland, a country in which women enjoy equal rights and responsibilities with men (and where a woman—Vigdis Finnbogadottir—has been elected President), suffered a significant loss of personal freedom and position when she married a man from Saudi Arabia. She was at first incredulous, then outraged, to discover that in some parts of today's world women really have no rights or independence, are cloistered from men, and are expected to wear face veils. She was forced by the society, more than by her husband, to adapt.

Milee, on the other hand, suffered from what she called too much liberty when she left the protected lifestyle of Vietnam for the wide open spaces of Australia, where she was "thrust out on [her] own," forced to learn to drive a car (which terrified her) and spend nights alone. She had to go out and around by herself

---

[16] *Ibid,* pp 70-71.

(made more frightening by her poor knowledge of English) and make major purchases and decisions during the many times her journalist husband was away on assignment. She talked of feeling betrayed and neglected, of being ashamed of her husband, who didn't know how to care for and protect his wife like a real man.

Harry, Milee's husband, was bewildered and annoyed by the helplessness of his timorous wife. He felt that she was "dumping total responsibility for her life and happiness on him, not pulling her own weight." He began to feel suffocated by her inability to adjust to Australian ways, by her clinging attachment to him, and by the totality of his responsibility. He needed a wife who was a partner and found himself with one who was a "stone around his neck."

Jaime also struggled with the battle between his personal beliefs regarding men's and women's roles and those which were the rule in the U.S. When Cassie had to find a part-time job to help them meet expenses (leaving him at home to care for Jennifer), he had a "hard time holding [his] head up." He was humiliated to be left with what in Santo Domingo would be considered women's work, with not being able to provide for his family, and with having to go against his principles by sending his wife out to work to augment his insufficient income. Worse still, he felt she was beginning to want to "wear the pants in the family" when she argued that she had as much right as he to decide what they were going to do with their combined salaries.

All of these spouses had expected their partners to be foreign reflections of their own preconceived notions of what a husband/wife should be. They had expected differences, even looked forward to them, but not in the basic role function. They felt betrayed by their spouses.

Of course, this is not always so. First of all, not every person adheres to the beliefs and behaviors of his or her own culture. Many have traveled and realize that their spouses have been raised within entirely different systems, and not everyone likes the way the male-female roles are assigned in their own countries. It could be that a woman from Iceland would want to escape from the responsibilities of her own culture and be willing to sacrifice some of her freedom in exchange for being taken care of. Harry might unconsciously want a submissive, dependent woman who is happy living within the confines of their home.

We are dealing with individuals; each story is different. What applies to one person is not necessarily true for another—even another of the same culture. Just because two people do not view the male/female roles identically does not mean they will not get along. The problem usually occurs when reality does not match expectations. For example, Milee expected Harry to be her savior. She did not expect him to "push her in and let her swim," and so she was disillusioned and disappointed, and her regard for him diminished. Had she understood his view of appropriate male/female role behavior, there would perhaps have been less of a problem.

When the man is from a male-dominant culture and the woman from an egalitarian one, the problem is usually greater than the other way around. Women in general, irrespective of culture, tend to be more relationship-oriented than men, and give more to keep the relationship going. But with a man who already considers women to be inferior, the woman generally has to give *much* more—and has to give up much more.

For Toronto-born Sara it wasn't so much the two hours a day preparing Joachim's lunch which bothered her as it was the fact that she had to give up her right to organize her own life as she saw fit. She was constantly "on call" to his wishes. She felt as though what she wanted didn't count any more, that she was valued only insofar as she adhered to his interpretation of what a good wife does.

Cassie felt that she had moved from being a free spirit to a subordinate and that she was being denied God-given (American) rights to her own freedom—to see whom she wanted, where and when, and to spend her own money as she saw fit.

Both women resented the unfamiliar and unexpected restraints; both men were upset and surprised that their women were so unfeminine and so unwilling to perform their roles as wives and mothers in the proper way.

On the other hand, where the couple lives often tempers their interpretation of their roles as men and women. When Yvette and Ali lived as fellow students in London, their relationship was that of comrades; each did his/her share in the flat and each respected the other's dedication to earning a degree. They helped one another towards that end.

But when they moved back to Kuwait, where male and female roles are clearly defined and adhered to, Ali felt obligated to dominate his foreign wife when his family and friends were around and to make her conform to the role of wife as it was seen in his culture. Yvette bristled under the unaccustomed bridle but was wise enough to defer to him in public. She made it quite clear, however, that she was not going to become a Kuwaiti wife in the privacy of their own home. It was not easy; Ali constantly received subtle pressures from his culture, unconsciously fell back into his old ways and viewpoints, and was torn between what he had been raised to expect and what his wife wanted. It was hard for Yvette to keep up the battle. But, as she said, it was easier to "keep on fighting" than to "face the fatigue of trying to live up to ideals and according to values not shared."

Sometimes cultures seem more similar than they really are and so the couples are truly unprepared for the subtle differences. Some unexpectedly difficult combinations are those between English and Americans, Danes and Swedes, and between Filipinos and Indonesians because these cultures which appear similar on the surface are really much more diverse than either partner imagines.

The male-female role issue is tied up with subtle and often intangible ideas regarding the meaning of marriage and intimacy, the necessity of companionship and mutual support, and of respect for one another as partners and individuals. This is a fundamental issue which must be sorted out because the spouse whose expectations have not been met usually feels betrayed, misunderstood, and perhaps even cheated out of what is "rightly" his or hers. The other partner has to live with feelings of deficiency and is apt to suffer a debilitating loss of self-esteem and may ultimately feel like a failure for not being able to live up to the spouse's ideals.

Italian Mario and his Irish wife Deirdre never saw eye-to-eye regarding the duties and privileges of the male/female roles and were never able to live up to each other's expectations. Mario wanted (and expected) a wife who gave him, as her first priority, not only his freedom to dally but her constant and unquestioning moral support and admiration merely because he fulfilled his obligations as successful wage earner and attentive father.

He felt that she did not "know how to be a wife," that she wanted " a friend instead of a husband." In fact Deirdre wanted someone who enjoyed her company, shared her dreams and supported her in her search for individual personal growth which, according to Mario, "was all nonsense for a woman." Because of their cultural biases, neither was able to fully comprehend, agree with, or satisfy the other's expectations of what a husband/wife should be.

Obviously, theirs was a personal as well as a cultural impasse, but their personal expectations of marriage were culturally infused. Each considered the other's way to be wrong. Both clung to what their own cultures taught.

Time

Time is the most valuable thing a man can spend.
—Theophrastus, "Diognes Laertius"
(from Lives of Eminent Philosophers)

When it is past in Paris, it is present in New York and future in Hong Kong...that is, if you are in New York.

We all know that there are different times all over the world. Anyone who has traveled over time zones has experienced jet lag—when one's body is not on the same time as one's watch. Many are vaguely aware that in different parts of the world the concept of time itself is different: that is, the meaning and value of time is different.

The question "How late is late?" will be answered differently from culture to culture. The notion of being on time will be assigned different importance. Some countries (the U.S., for instance) are more concerned with punctuality, with saving time, because they are countries based on future growth, and every moment counts towards building that future. Other countries (Hispanic or Arabic, for example) place more importance on *using* time than being on time; they believe in making the most of each moment by fully living it because culturally they are more interested in the quality of present life than in the future.

As a result, people in different parts of the world move at different paces. In Hispanic and Arabic cultures, for example, they are generally more relaxed and unhurried, engaging in time-consuming courtesies and ceremonies. To them interpersonal activities are more important than an external time clock. On the other hand, in the U.S. the emphasis is on productivity; time must be managed efficiently. People are in a hurry, often overlooking the interpersonal aspects of life.

"Tomorrow" means specifically the day after today in English, but becomes mañana in Spanish and *bukra* in Arabic, both of which refer to some undefined time in the future.

Anthropologist Edward T. Hall, in his studies on the cultural nature of time,[17] has found that different cultures move to different rhythmic patterns, and so do individuals. Individual rhythm is inherent, that is, it "begins in the center of the self."[18] Each person has his or her own sense of time and of speed and lives accordingly. But, each individual has also been trained to conform to certain cultural rhythms from the moment of birth. Each culture has been "choreographed in its own way, with its own beat, tempo and rhythm."[19] Thus, "While personality is undoubtedly a factor in interpersonal synchrony, culture is also a powerful determinant."[20] Though not every individual is in

[17] For more information on this topic, see Edward T. Hall, *The Dance of Life*.
[18] *Ibid,* p 181.
[19] *Ibid,* p 146.
[20] *Ibid,* p163.

sync with his or her own culture, people generally gauge themselves according to a central cultural time clock.

Frequently, people who marry outside their cultural group are incompatible with their own culture and more attuned to the rhythms of another—often that of the spouse, which might partially account for the attraction between the two. For example, an American who marries a Japanese might be someone who, while admiring progress, deplores the American way of tearing down the old to make way for the new and feels more attuned to a culture which venerates its elders, values its traditions, and preserves its heritage.

But, generally speaking, intercultural spouses are products of their own culture's time clock, which is frequently different from that of their partner. They have different unconscious rhythms and time patterns which can cause problems when they are trying to set up house together.

When these couples first meet, they are usually aware of such differences, but as they fall in love, the differences are temporarily suspended and each feels at one with the other. Only later, in the settling-in phase, do they tend to return to their own original rhythms and occasionally find that they are each moving to a different drummer. Perhaps one is always late, or the other is always in a hurry, or one doesn't want to waste time on little formalities which the other can't live without.

Occasionally, couples find that they are actually throwing each other off balance, but they don't know why. Many couples learn the other partner's rhythm and change their own, or they both adapt to the rhythm of the country where they live—insofar as it is physically possible. But there is an inner clock which does not change, and if these inner clocks are too different, the partners may find they are actually "unnerved by the stranger in the house who moves to a different beat," as German Helga experienced with her Libyan husband. "His time and my time are so different, that more and more we find we are doing things separately to avoid bickering. He resents my harping at him and says I try to keep track of his movements. He won't wear a watch, says he doesn't need it. For him time is rubber, it stretches. But I go mad when he says he's going out for fifteen minutes and comes back three hours later without any explanation. I have no schedules to work my day around, can never count on him to be on time for anything—movies, parties, even dinner. He is never *ever* on time for dinner. He believes in eating when he's hungry!"

Zoahar and Maria Clotilde (who met while he was an instructor at Club Med) explained their time difference problems in another way. "I work hard," says Zoahar, "and want to see the money I earn put aside for the future, see it grow, have the security a bank account can provide. She calls me stingy, uptight, says she doesn't care about the future—she'll be old then—she wants to have fun now. She quotes Octavio Paz at me: 'Whoever builds a house for future happiness, builds a prison for the present.[21] We argue about money constantly."

Joachim and Sara acknowledge that their lunch differences are based as much on differing ideas of time as anything else. Joachim, like most Portuguese, is used to a leisurely midday lunch and siesta. It isn't only that he resents Sara's not wanting to take the time to prepare his meal, he physically misses the break in the middle of the day—his body rebels. While Sara minds the imposition and is secretly disdainful of a man who wastes hours at the lunch table and sleeps half the afternoon away, she also finds that she can't ger her body to slow down and relax in the middle of the day. Although she has had to conform to the ways of the land, she still finds herself "sitting on the edge of the chair, waiting for the eternal meal to end, and pacing the floor waiting for everyone to wake up and get on with life."

As Sara found, the spouse who is living in the partner's country not only has to get in tune with his or her partner, but with the rhythms of the land. This definitely takes some extra adjustment.

The intercultural couple must remember that a spouse from one culture can be slowed down only so much, and a spouse from the other speeded up just so much before the strain shows. As with a record played at the wrong speed, the music is distorted.

[21] From *Posdata,* by poet Octavio Paz.

Place of Residence

Homesickness is... absolutely nothing. Fifty percent of the people in the world are homesick all the time... You don't really long for another country. You long for something in yourself that you don't have, or haven't been able to find.
—John Cheever, *The Stories of John Cheever*

By the very nature of the union, somebody in an intercultural marriage is the foreigner and has to learn to live and function in a foreign country (or they both do if they live in a third country). This spouse, despite how much affinity he or she may have for the new land (or lack of attachment to the homeland), will experience a degree of homesickness, i.e., loss of home and the security of a fully comprehended ambience. This will have an effect on their marriage.

The country where the couple lives will itself affect their relationship. Like it or not, the world outside the door will intrude on their marriage, be it his land, her land or a neutral third one. No matter what their individual cultures or the style they have chosen for their marriage, they will have dealings with the people of the country they are in and will have to respect its customs and values. They will have to observe the laws of the land and will be touched by the climate, the living conditions, the political situation, and the moral standards.

Finally, the pattern of life which the couple adopted in one country and which worked for them there will not necessarily function in another. Wherever the intercultural couple goes, there is adapting to be done, and adapting means effort and strain.

When Cecil met and married shy, pensive Ikumi, he had been living in Japan for three years, spoke the language, was familiar with and admired the ways of the land. He had studied Oriental art and poetry and was comfortable with Ikumi's friends and Asian cooking. The marriage was happy while they remained in Asia; the balance and style of the relationship remained the same.

When Cecil was recalled to England, Ikumi dutifully followed him. She had always known that the day would come when she would leave Japan, and she was anxious to see the world. In England, although their life changed in that they socialized much more and went on frequent outings and trips, Ikumi felt at ease among Cecil's friends, who were drawn mainly from an international crowd. Basically, she did what she had always done; only the locale was different.

However, when Cecil was posted to Bangladesh, everything changed for the couple, and the strain of life in that difficult country adversely affected their relationship. There they were both foreigners, without familiar friends and support systems, but also without the possibility of the kind of diversions they had enjoyed in their other postings; and each reacted to the life of hardship in a different way.

Cecil threw himself into sports, amateur theatrical activities and cocktail parties so loved by the British colonials as a means of survival "because there was nothing else to do." These, however, were not survival tactics familiar to Ikumi; she didn't care about these things, didn't share his feelings about the empire or the stiff upper lip. Instead, she withdrew from others, stopped eating, complained of headaches frequently, and became silent and remote, even from Cecil, who could not understand why she wouldn't try to adapt Eventually, she was diagnosed by an English doctor as being in the midst of a nervous breakdown and was advised to leave the country before it became more severe. With shame and sadness she returned to her parents in Japan to wait until Cecil finished his tour of duty.

Problems which stem from where the couple is living differ according to the people and the circumstances:

1. Some couples meet in the country of one of the partners and remain there. Thus, one is at home and the other is already familiar with the style of life in

that country and already functions there more or less successfully.

2.   Some meet in one country, marry and move to the country of the other. Most frequently (but certainly not always) it is the bride who follows her husband to his homeland and has to learn a whole new set of living patterns in order to function and be accepted in that country.

3.   Others meet and remain in or move to a country which is not home to either of them. Thus, both are expatriates, with the job not only of working out a marital style which incorporates their two cultures, but of adapting personally and as a couple to a third style. There are many couples who maintain that living in a third country is the only (or ideal) way for intercultural marriages to succeed.

Jaime chose to remain in the U.S., not only because of his attachment to Cassie, but because he believed the possibilities were better there for both of them and for their child. He also did not feel that Cassie could ever adjust to life in Santo Domingo and secretly feared she might not be accepted by his friends. He chose to accept the burden of being the one to adapt to the other culture.

Because she had never visited his country and had little understanding of his customs, Cassie had no way of truly appreciating the sacrifices he was making, nor of knowing just how far he had come in adapting to her ways. She accepted as natural the fact that their friends were almost all drawn from her friends, that their daily fare was American food and their language English. She made no real effort to learn Spanish or become familiar with any of his customs. She saw no need. Because he didn't complain, she thought it was easy for him and assumed, therefore, that he (as well as she) knew that American ways were better. Not until they made friends with another intercultural couple did she realize how well Jaime was coping with living in the U.S. and began to see the effort he was making.

The spouse who is the foreigner is normally the one who has to make the most adjustments, which is fine if the foreigner likes and admires the culture of the spouse; it is miserable if not. The expatriate spouse is isolated from familiar support systems, friends and family, and is disadvantaged in the marital power struggle. The home spouse, on the other hand, is surrounded by constant cultural reinforcements in the form of a familiar lifestyle and familiar objects and customs, as well as old friends. The home spouse usually feels less need to alter familiar ways and expects the foreign spouse to fit in.

Probably the most difficult adjustment has to be made by the couple which meets in one spouse's country, sets up a pattern of living and then moves to the other's country. This is an especially difficult problem if the new expatriate doesn't know what to expect and is faced with substandard living conditions, repressive laws, human rights violations, difficult climate, political unrest, manifest poverty or hunger, or a religion which dominates the lifestyles of whoever lives there. Simply knowing about these difficulties does not prepare people for the harsh reality of learning how to live with them. The external stress can interfere with the couple's relationship and bring about tensions which will strain it.

Whatever the conditions in the country, the move itself may affect the relationship. Any change is difficult and stirs deep anxieties, often at an unconscious level. The couple won't really know why they are suddenly tense or aggressive with one another and will look to anything or anyone to lay the blame on. Their world gets shuffled. What worked for them before often has to be reworked in light of the ways of the new culture. Not only does the foreign spouse have new customs, living conditions and often a new language to adjust to, but also both spouses often have to mold a new kind of personal relationship to suit the new land. The apple cart has been upset and they have to start over again. Perhaps the most upsetting and thorny problem is that the spouse often goes through significant personality changes upon returning home, reassuming old, familiar roles.

Rosemary, an American, who had met and married her Indian husband Ravi while both were on a training program in Toronto, was fascinated by him and everything Indian while they were in Canada. She studied Indian history, art, language, and cooking in her enthusiasm to embrace his culture. She wore a sari whenever she entertained his many Indian friends and family who visited Toronto.

But the allure wore off when they moved to New Delhi and she saw her urbane, sophisticated husband become absorbed back into his old culture, which gradually transformed him. She nervously watched as the more passive (and in Canada, repressed) aspects of his character began to re-emerge. She felt isolated as he bowed to his mother's will, even in matters which she felt concerned only them as a couple; he rarely defended her from critical scrutiny or openly took her part. It was as though he were the prodigal son returned home, who put on his old clothes and erased the past years—the life they had had together.

Rosemary, who already had her hands full adjusting to the move and to this different life, felt that Ravi was pulling away from her, falling out of love. She began to lose her self-confidence and, instead of learning to cope better as time went on, began to function less well and to hate India for what it was doing to her marriage. She counted the days until they could move somewhere—anywhere—else. Luckily for them, Ravi was eventually given another assignment, this time in Germany. Far from the eyes and influence of his own culture, Ravi readopted the ways Rosemary had known when they fell in love, and gradually things returned to normal.

On the other hand, Carol had been happy with life in Chile. She had been working in the U.S. embassy there when she met Miguel and had submitted willingly enough to the Chilean way of life, even to the male-dominant arrangement in their marriage, and she had the understanding of her colleagues at the embassy.

But when Carol was reposted to Washington, D.C., and Miguel agreed to follow, that arrangement no longer worked for them. She was embarrassed by his demanding and bossy ways in front of her old friends, and she began to feel the subtle pressure of other Americans, who wondered aloud how she could put up with "being treated like a doormat, a second-class citizen."

Miguel never ceased to praise Chile and attack his wife's country and countrymen. He berated the U.S. government for its position regarding Chile; he criticized her friends and compatriots as "classless boors"; he disdained the kind of food offered to them in the homes of American acquaintances and insisted on his native cuisine in their own home; he was suspicious of her friends and work associates and insisted on befriending only other Hispanics; and he blatantly and openly boasted he was in America "only for the money." As she maneuvered for a new position in the marriage, he reacted with anger, berating her for becoming a "rampant feminist," an "emasculating woman."

Although he loved Carol and had followed her to the U.S. to be with her, he hated her culture and wasn't going to meet her halfway in any kind of compromise. Like someone who doesn't distinguish between the map and the territory, he began to identify her with everything about her country he didn't like. She began to feel as though they had made an Hispanic ghetto out of their home in her own country, and she resented having to compromise her cultural heritage to please him—or, rather, to attempt to please him. The roles which had worked in Chile didn't in Washington. If the marriage was to be saved, the patterns of their relationship had to be modified.

Finding mutual friends, difficult enough when one partner is a foreigner, is often more so in countries where both partners are outsiders.[22] Isabella from Madrid and Josef from Leningrad, who chose Paris because of the international character of that city, were fortunate to find themselves surrounded by expatriates from their own countries. Even so, they admitted to a nagging nostalgia for the countries and families they had left behind and to some regrets at having to become expatriates, especially since their children, who were growing up French, knew next to nothing about their parents' cultures and spoke neither of their languages.

[22] More in section headed "Friends," p 64.

Politics

All religions, laws, moral and political systems are but necessary means to preserve social order.
>—Ch'en Tu-hsiu,"The New Youth "
>(from *Sources of Chinese Tradition,*
>William Theodore De Bary, ed.)

At first glance politics would seem to have little to do with love and marriage, but in intercultural marriages it intrudes if (1) the partners adhere to fundamentally different political philosophies; (2) they are forced to live in a different country because of the political situation in the land or because of the beliefs or practices of one of the partners; or (3) they live in a country which is in a state of war.

Just as it is unusual for two people who are zealous adherents of entirely different and mutually exclusive religions to marry, so it is unusual for partners who are each sincerely adamant believers in opposing political philosophies. This is not to say that it can't happen, but the more usual scenario is for at least one of the two to be politically flexible, open-minded or even indifferent, giving way to the persuasion of the more dominant one—or for both to live and let live. For example, Brazilian Maria Clotilde, to use her own words, "couldn't have cared less" about global affairs unless they touched on her daily life, while her husband Zoahar was a dedicated pacifist who devoted his professional and personal time to working and marching for human rights and other causes. One partner acted as a balance to the other, and they were perfectly compatible in their different attitudes toward politics.

Some couples seem politically farther apart than they really are. Italian Communist Party member, Fiamma, bejeweled and befurred (from head to toe), was more verbally opposed (for the shock value her ideologies caused in bourgeois circles) to the capitalist views of her English husband, Andrew, than she was in actuality; she never permitted the party line to interfere with the jet-set lifestyle his millions provided. Andrew, on the other hand, admittedly believed in nothing; he considered all governments equally corrupt and was amused by his "comrade wife in mink" who alternately defended the rights of the worker and sent back the wine at the Tour d'Argent.

Couples with sincere political differences, however, can have problems. Chilean Miguel and American Carol, for example, were both politically involved and poles apart in their beliefs. It was useless for them to say they were going to keep politics out of their marriage. They eventually felt the strain, whichever country they lived in, and they inevitably tangled over the issues.

In Chile, even though Carol had managed to accommodate to the Chilean lifestyle, she still worked for the American embassy representing her country, and she found it difficult to reconcile that with her association with Miguel and his anti-American friends. Her boss also was not pleased with her impending marriage to a "high-risk, host country national," and his friends were unhappy to lose one of their own to an imperialist. Opposition came at them from all angles.

Much as they tried to keep encounters purely social, politics crept in. They had to meet either her friends or his friends. His friends baited her, and while she listened to their point of view, she also felt obligated to defend her country's position and voice her opinion of human rights violations. Often tempers flared and feelings were hurt. More and more Miguel and Carol went out alone together, isolating themselves in order to avoid conflict, which both of them regretted whenever it occurred.

Miguel began to be ostracized by his more radical companions, and Carol started to avoid her American friends. As much as they told themselves that having to overcome these obstacles to be together would only strengthen their love, the sacrifices were hard on them.

To a certain extent intercultural spouses marry the fate of their partner's land. Helga, the youthful rebel, the German-born wife of the Libyan activist, was eventually forced to leave Libya with her children and live in Switzerland because of her husband's political activities. Although she dropped many of her own radical views and activities once she moved to Tripoli and had children, she was not able to escape Libyan politics. Living in Tripoli was dangerous. In addition, her husband was always involved in some underground activity. Sometimes days went by when Helga didn't hear from him, and she began to panic. She knew better than to ask questions, but she often combed the hospitals and prisons, placing money in the right hands, for information when he had been out of touch for longer than usual. She lived in constant fear for him and for herself and her children.

The toll began to wear her down and shatter her nerves. Finally her husband packed her off with their children to Switzerland to wait for a political change, so that they could be together again either in his homeland or hers. So she waited alone, married but without her husband, in limbo, waiting for a man whose life was totally entwined with his country's political situation.

Helga is but one of many intercultural spouses to find themselves living in third countries because of politics, but some are not simply waiting for their spouses; they are outcasts, often permanent outcasts.

Josef and Isabella, for example, knew they would never be able to go back to his native Russia because he had escaped (using a false passport and leaving everything behind) and would be imprisoned if he tried to return. Although he was outspoken in his anti-Communist views, he loved his country and missed it. Isabella experienced a phenomenon quite common in intercultural marriage: being identified with the spouse's nationality in the eyes of strangers. Despite the fact that Josef was adamantly anti-Communist, and that she, despite her Russian surname, was not even Russian, both of them were often taunted as "Commie pigs" by anti-Communists. They were both incorrectly labeled and judged and were sometimes persecuted accordingly.

Their case is not unusual. Adela and Mohammed, who met and married in Philadelphia, were attracted to one another in part by the similarity of their homeless condition; one was a refugee from Cuba, the other, from Iran. Depending on which country was in the news at the time, they suffered alternately from the anti-Cuban and anti-Iranian prejudices of people although they were in Philadelphia precisely because they did not agree with what was going on in their countries and felt compelled to leave. When the American Embassy was taken in Teheran, for example, they received anonymous phone calls threatening them or their children. Fear became a daily emotion.

As Adela said, "It was hard enough for both of us to have to live in a country not our own, far away from those we had left behind, worrying about their well-being and their safety, trying to earn extra money to send back to arrange for their exits, living our lives in one land but attached with invisible ties and loyalties to the ones we left. But to be identified with our enemies was almost unbearable."

The political situation also affected the lives of Harry and Milee. After the fall of Saigon, they were not at peace until they had managed to assist her family in relocating to Australia, which meant actually taking in her entire family (mother, father, siblings, and grandmother) and assuming responsibility for their travel expenses, clothing and food, and for finding them jobs, homes, and schools. Over a ten-year period, two or three of her Vietnamese relatives at a time lived with them, draining their finances, straining their intimate family lifestyle. Harry found himself "surrounded by a foreign colony" which spoke a language he didn't speak and cooked food he didn't like in what was left of his own home. He and Milee often took long walks just to be alone together.

Although he did not regret what they did, he was glad when it was over and he and his wife were on their own, finally able to permit themselves a few extras: a new car, a family vacation, a bank account with something in it.

The adjustment of the intercultural couple is also affected by the political climate of their chosen country. If this climate includes instability, civil war, racial tension, terrorist activities, a violent or repressive government, the marriage may be in for some hard times.

When Deirdre married Mario, it never occurred to her that life would be much different. After all, she was going to a Western European country, and when they moved to Rome in the 1970s, she was more than enthusiastic about the life she led. The few inconveniences—the strikes which regularly stopped essential services, the student protests, the occasional terrorist attacks on public places—seemed a small price to pay for living in that beautiful country. None of it really touched her deeply: "A little tear gas here and there, but I got used to it," was how she explained it.

But like Helga in Libya, after their children were born, these things bothered her more, and the tension increased. She actually knew one or two of the people who were kidnapped; a friend of theirs was a victim of an airport bomb; and the children went to the American school on buses which were inspected daily by armed police and specially trained dogs. Fear became a common companion; people stopped going out much; the streets were deserted by 10:30 at night; the women put away their furs and stopped carrying handbags for fear of being accosted; and the men were armed with guns.

It wasn't fun anymore, and gradually the situation began to wear on her nerves and on Mario's (who went to work at the bank in an armored car, taking a different route every day so as not to be a target for an unknown, unseen assailant). They, their children, and their friends lived in a controlled but constant state of tension. They were afraid to pick up the newspaper for fear of reading about the latest public outrage. Some people left the country; others got their money across the border into Switzerland. Uncertainty became their daily diet, and Deirdre began to wonder whether it was worth it.

Life in other countries with repressive but stable governments poses other kinds of problems for the intercultural spouse. Living where the people are not free to move around as they like, where dissenters whisper their conversations for fear of being overheard, where telephones are monitored and mail is opened, and where newspapers are censored and homes randomly searched can be suffocating, especially to someone raised in a free country.

As Italian diplomat Massimo and his Danish wife Tove found when they were posted to Beijing, the ability to adapt to a politically repressive environment depends on the personal makeup of the individual and much on how long they have to stay. Anyone can stand it for a while, but after three years, one's sense of humor and sense of good sportsmanship wane and life drags interminably from one vacation, one home leave, to the next.

Friends

The fortunate man has bread and friends.

—Korean Proverb

Friendship is a basic need of human beings. Finding a friend, someone with whom one has shared sensibilities is important, even within one's own culture. In many respects it parallels the marital relationship in that its success depends on two people having the same background, interests and values. All cultures value friendship, and all couples need friends, but finding and maintaining them often presents unique problems for intercultural couples.

The reasons are many. For one thing, cultures have their own definitions of what constitutes friendship and different rules regarding fostering and maintaining them. Americans, for example, easily make (and often just as easily discard) friends. Many Europeans associate only within their own social circles. Latin Americans and Middle Easterners consider friends as people who can be counted on for anything, who will never let them down.

Another problem commonly experienced by intercultural couples is that, while they themselves may have adjusted to the many cultural differences between them, their friends may not have been able or willing to and may be uncomfortable around the foreign partner. Finally, one or both of the spouses may not like or be comfortable with the other's friends and may not only want to avoid them personally but may also object to the time given them by their partner.

Finding a way to overcome these problems is critical because having friends is important not only for the individuals but for the marriage itself. An isolated couple is neither a happy nor a healthy one. Friends are needed not only as an outlet or cushion for moments of stress or conflict, which even the happiest marriages encounter, but also to keep the partners from becoming too isolated or dependent on one another, which may eventually come to mean having too much of each other's company.

While Yvette and Ali were living in London, they both had friends of many nationalities drawn from the foreign student population of the university; nevertheless, as a couple they associated primarily with Ali's friends. Yvette had French women friends whom she saw alone. Basically, it was a satisfactory arrangement.

Ali's friends were invariably courteous to her and fun to be around. If she had any complaint, it was that they were around a little too much—she and Ali had little time alone together. But she accepted Ali's explanation that in his culture, people don't apply time limits (or any other kind of limits) to friendships. As Yvette saw it, this meant no privacy and no personal property—what was theirs was everyone's. This was not an easy thing for her to accept, but she felt guilty and selfish complaining about it.

When Ali finished his degree, they married and moved to Kuwait, where Yvette was thrown off balance by being suddenly deprived of the outlet provided by her women friends who saw things the same way she did and by being just as suddenly surrounded by people who saw the world as Ali did.

In addition, she found that many of the same men who had camped in their apartment in London and who had interacted with her freely, now treated her with deference, ignoring her after the first social amenities and leaving her to the women—who, for the most part, bored her. "They are sweet," she said, "I just have nothing to say to them, and they have never really accepted me as one of them either."

The need for a close same-sex friend, "someone with whom to share impressions of what I was experiencing in this new country, someone who would understand my doubts, fears, problems, as well as my enthusiasms," was a need expressed by Rosemary as well during her years in India. Ravi was going through reentry shock and wrestling with the changes demanded of him as he readapted to India, and both of them were struggling with what it meant to their relationship. Feeling distanced from him, she had no one to turn to or confide in. She also bemoaned the difficulty they had in finding couples they both could relate to. "There were intercultural couples where we were living, but although the wives were foreign and the husbands Indian, the women were rarely from my same background or nationality, and the men were not often from the same Indian subculture as my husband. So, in the end we had little in common."

Dorrie, with the fair complexion and blond hair so typical of her Dutch compatriots, also experienced isolation when she and her Japanese husband returned to Tokyo after she finished her graduate degree. "Because we Western women so obviously look different, we stand out and in reality are left out," she explained. "In our case, because Hiroshi and I both moved in the academic world, I was accepted but being accepted is not the same thing as having a good close friend. I personally like to be open and informal and find that I cannot—*must* not—be myself in Japan. After a while that gets tiresome and I long for the casual kind of relationships I can have with people of my own country."

Many couples find that their same-culture friends are uncomfortable around their spouses and sometimes disapprove of the marriage. Even when the friends have accepted the marriage, they often still feel awkward around the other partner and don't know what to say. The situation is further complicated if there is a language barrier. The friends must slow down, repeat, and explain, which makes for stilted socializing. Worse yet, they sometimes simply ignore the foreigner's presence which causes resentment.

Jaime often became angry with Cassie and her friends when they laughed and joked together, not always taking care to be sure he had understood. He got to the point where he stopped trying and tuned them out, and so he was only half there when her friends were around. He was unable to accept Cassie's defense of her friends—that they were uncomfortable around him because they weren't sure he liked or approved of them.

"It wasn't just a problem of language," Jaime explained. "We had different interests and different points of view. You need someone like yourself to ward off the feelings of isolation, someone who shares your ideas, especially when you are the outsider in a country."

Jaime also had problems with Cassie's insistence on keeping her former male friends. Much as he tried to believe her claim that "in Chicago men and women can be *just* friends," it went against his nature; he didn't like it, and he didn't want his wife doing it. But he felt alone in taking this position, outnumbered and disadvantaged in defending his viewpoint, which, of course, he resented. As a result, he became even more convinced he was right, more determined to win "at least this one." It was one of the issues they never really resolved.

Vietnamese Milee also admitted quite frankly that she did not have any real friends who were not Asian-born: "I like the Australians, but they cannot be my true friends. We are too different." At first Harry was upset by her failure to integrate fully into life in Australia and form any close friendships among his people; but at the same time he was relieved when she finally met a Japanese woman who introduced her to a group of other Asian wives because he saw how badly she needed their companionship. Then, of course, as her family arrived from Vietnam, she associated primarily with them.

Not only could Milee not relate to Harry's blunt, outspoken friends, she had problems understanding Harry's way of relating to his own friends. She resented the touching and hugging that went on between men and women, finding it distasteful and unnecessarily intimate. She had trouble accepting the way he "mistreated" his good friends when they were guests in their home, engaging in loud, frank arguments, pointed, intrusive questions, sarcasm and teasing, which she found totally lacking in sensitivity and courtesy.

Many couples find that they get along best with other international couples, not only because they share some of the same experiences and problems, but because they are better able to understand and empathize with the delicate and difficult balance both couples have managed to achieve in their marriages. Both couples usually know how not to intrude and also can serve as sounding boards for one another, sharing the mutuality of problems not experienced by the average couple.

Like Yvette and Rosemary, Rashida was touched by the sincere open warmth of the women, but she knew she was not like them and felt separate. She depended a great deal on her friendship with other Afro-American wives, who, like her, had married Kenyan men. "We were life-savers to one another, talked the same shorthand and shared the common bond of nationality and the common experience of being frequently in a state of frustration and confusion. We were truly sisters." Their husbands benefited as well from being able to share with one another their experiences with these foreign wives.

Friendship is often a big issue for international couples and, in some ways, one that causes frequent tangles. Perhaps the ideal solution, such as that found by Milee and Harry, is for both partners to have "lots of different kinds of friends. I have my friends," Harry explained, "and she has her friends, and we have our friends. Sometimes we get together with the husbands of her friends or the wives of my friends, or have 'Esperanto' parties all together. We don't both get along with everyone, but that's all right because each of us separately and both of us together have managed, with some trial and error, to fill in the gaps."

Finances

Money is the sinew of love as well as of war.
>   —Thomas Fuller, *Gnomonologia*

In all marriages, monocultural and intercultural alike, money issues are a source of major conflict. But financial problems are often more numerous and tougher to solve in intercultural marriages because of culturally-based differences regarding such matters as who should earn the money and who controls its expenditure; how much should be spent and how much saved; and what kinds of things it should be spent on (personal pleasures, children, relatives, etc.). There are different value orientations involved and different priorities to be considered by intercultural partners, and it may take more money to keep such a marriage going smoothly because of the diverse needs and desires of the partners.

Who earns the money in the family can be a male-female role issue. In some cultures—even where they have newly-won legal rights to control their property—women have little say in managing finances and are totally dependent upon their husbands and must ask their permission for every expense.

Earning money is often an exclusively male role. In Latin cultures the traditional husband wants his wife at home, and, although today the necessity of two-income families is breaking down this type of sexism, it has not disappeared.

Mario, for example, did everything he could to sabotage Deirdre's attempts to pick up the career she had left when she married and followed him to Italy. "The evils of the world stem from the woman who works," he told her, implying that she would inevitably fail in her true role as wife and mother if she were to return to work.

Even Jaime, who recognized that they couldn't get by without Cassie's paycheck, felt less a man because of his working wife and promised himself that as soon as he got a decent job he would make her stop and stay home with Jennifer.

Sune, on the other hand, who came from Sweden where women tote their own burdens, was often frustrated at being the sole wage earner; but he was never able to convince his Malaysian wife, Rani, that she might help out. She was shocked that he was not proud to be able to support a wife who stayed at home. She had not been prepared to do anything else. For her, working was out of the question.

Sometimes the argument is over how much money is saved and how much spent immediately. Although this issue depends for the most part on the individual personalities involved, it can also be a cultural issue. In some cultures people live for the present and in others, for the future—which affects whether they are more interested in enjoying their money today or saving for tomorrow.

Maria Clotilde and Zoahar were typical examples of their cultural types. As a good Brazilian carioca, she knew that life was to be lived and enjoyed and had little patience with her Israeli husband, Zoahar, who came home too tired at the end of the day to want to do more than eat and sleep. She saw no point in someone working so hard that he didn't have the time or energy left to enjoy the money his work produced.

But Zoahar had known poverty and insecurity and felt that a good bank account was his only defense against the unknown future. He found her attitude frivolous and kept close tabs on how she spent the money he doled out to her. They had very different ideas of what to do with their money, even regarding essentials like food, clothing and housing. What she considered essentials, he considered extras. She felt life was not worth living without dining out and dancing; he thought these were frivolities. While she spent money on hairdressers, dressmakers and phone calls to her friends and family in Rio de Janeiro, he made donations to political or charitable causes and invested in growth stocks. Their arguments rarely ceased.

A common intercultural issue stemming from how money should be spent is that of the extent of financial responsibility a spouse feels for friends and extended family. Milee and Harry were fortunate in that he understood that she had a filial duty to her parents, instilled in her by her culture, and that she would never be happy, no matter how much money they had to spend on themselves, until her family was safely settled close by her. Telling himself it would not be forever, he made her priorities his and worked to help her family until all of them were safe. Still, there were times when he wondered when they would be able to use his hard-earned money for themselves.

Even though Adela as a Cuban understood and shared her Iranian husband's sense of loyalty to his family and friends, she resented the fact that there were no limits placed on what they could afford to share and that there was rarely any money left over for themselves. The others always came first—there was always another brother to put through school. She felt that his Iranian friends took advantage of him as well and finally persuaded him to curtail some of his monetary assistance. As a result, some of his friends turned against him, feeling that he had betrayed them and that he had been contaminated by the American culture in which he lived.

Cecil understood Ikumi's need to return home, to be with her family and friends, and felt that the money for her frequent trips was money well spent. But when their first child was ready for higher education, there was not enough to support both her trips and an expensive boarding school. Despite her lamentations that she did not want the boy to go away from home for school, the English boarding school won out.

Deirdre also felt that trips home, to touch base with her culture and to be with her friends and family, took priority in their budgeting, but Mario insisted on the more luxurious status vacations which enabled him to maintain *bella figura* among his friends.

Olu took it as one more sign that his wife was not a proper woman when she complained that her own paycheck was used to help out his extended family—a matter about which she was given little say. Things became even more tense when their sons (under their mother's tutelage) questioned why the grandmothers and cousins were given preference over them.

When money is unlimited, the priorities of both partners can generally be satisfied (both partners willing), but when it is not, there are choices to be made. As Dorrie put it, "Every foreign spouse should have some 'hesso-kuri,' which literally translates as 'honorable funds hidden in belly button,' for psychological independence, for emergencies, travel to homeland, medical problems, and also, of course, in case the marriage ends in divorce."

In-Laws

In my very own self, I am part of my family.
—D.H. Lawrence, *Apocalypse*

Families are not something young men and women shed upon marrying, but usually something they acquire more of. In an intercultural marriage, not only do they get a set of foreign in-laws but may also wed a totally absorbing concept of family, which will have a great bearing on how they live their married lives.

In certain cultures (for example Anglo-Saxon, Scandinavian), parents normally begin educating their children at an early age to accept responsibility for their actions and then push them out of the nest as soon as they can stand on their own two feet, expecting them to resolve their own problems. They avoid invading their children's privacy once they have reached adulthood, and they themselves often settle into retirement colonies or old people's homes when they are no longer able to care for themselves.

In other cultures (Asian, Middle Eastern, African, for example) parents never really let go of their children. They maintain patriarchal authority and do not expect to be abandoned in their old age. They devote themselves to their children when they are small but have power over them and expect eternal respect and loyalty from them when they are grown. The family tie does not decrease, but extends when a son or daughter marries.

These cultural differences make for quite different interpretations of how to handle and relate to in-laws. More often than in monocultural marriages, parents may strongly disapprove of the child's choice of a spouse. While initially pulling the couple closer in mutual self-defense, parental opposition in the long run can precipitate conflict and distrust.

Even before marriage, in-laws can pose a threat to the couple. When Cecil and Ikumi decided to marry, her family was devastated and did everything in its power to break up the relationship. Despite Cecil's upright character and good position, the parents looked upon the marriage of their daughter to a foreigner as an unforgivable act, which would bring shame on the family. At one point they controlled their daughter's movements to keep the couple from meeting and tried to pay Cecil to leave the country.

This reaction, while extreme, is not rare for parents of intercultural couples. Bill and Mary experienced the same kind of resistance to their marriage from both sets of parents. His family had accepted and understood Bill's involvement in civil rights issues during and after his college days and had even encouraged his involvement in the Peace Corps. But they felt he had gone too far when he brought home a bride who was not only from another country (Nigeria) but of another race, and they could not accept the marriage. Mary's family was no less horrified. To them the world was divided into black and white, and she had joined the enemy. They wanted no part of the young couple.

Even when the families have accepted the marriage there is often a stand-off period while they wait to see how well the new son- or daughter-in-law will conform to their ways. They often take subtle (or not so subtle) measures designed to influence the behavior of the newlyweds, often undermining the solidity of the young couple's unity.

Rosemary, for example, waged a continuing battle with her mother-in-law over the question of Ravi's primary allegiance.

While she understood—abstractly—that his culture called for stronger ties to his family and greater deference to his mother's will than her own American culture, when it took precedence over their personal relationship, she resented and fought it. She also struggled to retain her independence from her mother-in-law, who attempted to transform her into an exemplary, subservient Indian daughter-in-law. This constant tug-of-war posed many problems for the couple during their years in India and was resolved only by their transfer out of the country.

The family can, of course, also be the couple's best ally, its staunchest supporter, willing to help when needed, and strong when the couple is having problems. Yvette found that the women of Ali's family secretly admired and envied her egalitarian relationship with her husband and encouraged her to maintain it within their own culture. "My mother-in-law is a closet feminist, Yvette confided, "and while I find that I don't have a lot to say to her and her daughters beyond home and family, their warmth and 'secret support' have more than compensated for it."

Even Ali's father accepted her ways—as long as she bowed to his absolute authority over the entire family. If she respected their ways, she found them very accepting; they were delighted to teach her their customs, their cooking, and to help out whenever needed. "I have been enveloped in the warmth of their understanding, acceptance and kindness, which has helped me overcome inevitable bouts of homesickness."

Milee, on the other hand, had a problem with the exuberant warmth and welcome she received from Harry's Australian family. While she understood the sincerity of their manners, these were not her ways and instinctively she drew back and unwittingly offended them. Harry found himself acting as a constant go-between, explaining to his family that her reserve was not repugnance and explaining to her that their teasing was not meant to be hurtful or rude.

Close family involvement can also smother or burden an intercultural marriage, particularly when one partner is not used to a close and demanding family relationship.

Jaime's family was initially unable to fully accept Cassie or to understand her reasons for putting off marrying him. They felt that as the mother of his child, she had to marry him and the fact that she wanted to wait until she was sure that he was marrying her for herself, not "out of some dumb Latin sense of duty," was beyond their comprehension. But when they did marry, all was forgiven and Cassie became a member of the family—with all the good and bad that involved.

After the marriage, a stream of Jaime's relatives began to arrive in Chicago for prolonged stays, which not only strained the couple's meager budget but put an almost unbearable strain on their relationship. Jaime placed no limits on their welcome, nor on how much he did for them. He became a different person, as far as Cassie could see, when they were around, reverting to the macho behavior expected of a man in his culture, and requiring behavior from Cassie which had nothing to do with the kind of relationship they had established. The presence of these resident relatives threw their entire relationship out of kilter, changed the atmosphere of their home, and frayed their tempers.

Olu's parents were wonderful to American Rashida when she came to live in Kenya; and though she had trouble learning to accept their practice of interference in any or all of the couple's affairs, she found that they were able to mediate the arguments between the two of them just as much as they often unwittingly caused them. But it went against her grain to be ruled by her in-laws and to accept that her husband felt his duties to his family came before his duties to his wife and sons.

Some couples find that their marital survival depends on the distance they keep from both sets of in-laws and so choose to live in a third country, where they are free to live their own lives and resolve their own problems. But running away, as some couples view it, can be a lonely, incomplete answer, because it doesn't really resolve anything. Both spouses cut themselves off from not only their pasts but from their support systems and often find that, as time passes, they have to deal with worries and problems of what to do with elderly parents who may become ill or infirm.

Mary, who lived in Berkeley, California, far from her parents in Nigeria, knew the desperation of being distant from loved ones when she learned that her father had fallen ill and that his days were numbered.

Her brothers and sisters said "Come now," but that was impossible. Mary's daughter was in the hospital and needed her. It was no use saying Bill could take over; he had a full-time job, one which took him all over the country. There was no extended family to fall back on as there would have been in Nigeria, no one who could help out. Her duties were *here,* now, to her immediate family.

"Tell him to wait," she begged her mother over the phone. "I'll get there somehow. Don't let him die." She was torn between her responsibilities.

In Mary's case her father did hang on until she was able to reach his bedside weeks later, but some expatriate spouses never see their parents again, and this can be one of their greatest sacrifices.

In sum, close family involvement is a double-edged sword; the extended family can be the couple's best ally or the couple's worst enemy, confusing involvement with interference, invading the couple's privacy, and perhaps even instigating arguments and causing problems. Although some couples are bonded more closely as a reaction against nonsupportive parents, others claim that external problems which arise because of the family of one or the other cause them more conflict than any other issue.

Social Class

A man's manners are a mirror in which he shows his portrait.
—Goethe, *Proverbs in Prose*

Some people maintain, even some intercultural couples, that there is nothing more complicated or difficult about intercultural marriage than there is about a monocultural one as long as both partners come from the same social strata of their respective societies.

While this is an oversimplification of the matter, it is true that class counts. Similar social background is an important ingredient in any marriage, whether intercultural or not. However, there seems to be more class-crossing in intercultural marriages than in monocultural ones. There are various explanations for this, many of them tied to the motivations behind the marriage. Rebels, for example (remember our typologies in the first chapter), tend to be reacting against their cultures or their personal backgrounds in choosing their spouses. But more often it is a matter of ignorance: the participants often aren't aware of the class differences. They simply don't know enough about their partner's culture to be able to assess his or her status within it. Often one (or both, in the case of couples who meet in third countries) of the partners has never been to the other's country to see the culture in action; therefore, he/she has no idea what is and isn't acceptable behavior in the other's society and so attributes a lot of questionable behavior to foreignness, rather than to class difference.

As Yvette explained it, "I forgave him all sorts of things I'd never let a French guy get away with because I thought that was just the way they did things in his country. Was I mad when I found out that in some ways he was a boor even in his own language."

Frequently the failure to recognize class differences happens because the young people meet as students on neutral ground in a third country where they are foreigners, coping with the ways of a land which is strange to both of them, making mistakes and sometimes expressing themselves haltingly and incorrectly, sometimes in a language neither of them speaks fluently.

Often they meet on a university campus where a student ghetto-like atmosphere prevails: everyone dresses alike and uses the same, currently popular modes of expression and behavior, which might be quite different from what they would use at home. There may be little real interaction with adults other than the university personnel (who don't count, as they reflect the student styles as well). When the couple meet, both are playing the role of student and are often quite different people from what they are at home.

When they return to their own countries, they revert to familiar roles, habits and patterns of behavior. The bride or groom they brought with them may be in for a few surprises. The family may not be what had been portrayed. In their limbo-like courtship neither one of them probably gave—or was able to give—an accurate description of what "back home" was like.

Much the same thing happens when servicemen marry women of the country where they are stationed. Often loneliness overcomes common sense, and the soldier marries the first woman he meets, knowing next to nothing about her or the culture of her country. The woman often doesn't have any real idea about his family or background until they return to his homeland and she sees him out of uniform and interacting with his relatives and friends.

One Korean war bride who ended up in the heart of Kansas was so distressed by what she had done that upon arrival in her husband's modest, isolated home, she took to her room and didn't eat or leave it for a week. In time the innate kindness of the family won her over, but she had to learn to live in a social setting and with people of educational background different from her own and to associate with a class of people she would never have known in her own land.

Visiting the spouse's country may not help either, since the partner often does not speak the language (or doesn't speak it well) and so misses telltale speech patterns, accents and grammatical slipups, which would give some indication of social background. Even those who have spent some time in their spouse's homeland and have some knowledge of the language have only been visitors and so have had few intimate contacts with the people. As a result, their understanding of status delineations or subtle class distinctions is likely to be severely limited, and they will often totally miss those aspects of their prospective partner's speech and behavior which would give them the clues they need. It takes time to figure out where people really belong in another society because each culture has its own set of rules and its own fine lines of distinction; it is hard to tell where cultural customs end and social delineations begin.

The situation is further complicated by the fact that certain class attributes in one culture may not be shared by the same class in another. For example, cleanliness in North America might be called a middle-class value, but it is not shared by the middle classes in some other countries. What is considered decent dress or courteous behavior by a certain class in one culture may or may not hold for the same class in another. Unfortunately, the foreigner may never know for sure.

Class difference is one of the biggest causes of conflict in intercultural marriage, as in any marriage, because it carries over into so many other areas. The way someone blows his nose, chews his food, sits or stands in public, or interacts with peers has as much to do with family, educational and social background as it does with nationality. These class-determined behaviors are the very fabric of daily life. Social background will determine not only the behavior of each of the spouses, but also their attitudes towards many other things that will be part of their lives together: sex, education, work, recreation, financial management, leisure activities, role definitions (the division of chores as well as the freedom of women), etc.

Although class is one of the major issues in an intercultural marriage, it is often overlooked as a culprit when things begin to go wrong: usually the cultural differences get blamed instead— "She does this or that because of her Yugoslav/Moroccan/ English, etc., background." In a roundabout way this is true— the culture difference is to blame, probably because the couple made the error of marrying across class *because* they were foreign to one another and didn't perceive their class differences. They probably wouldn't have made the same mistake with someone from their own culture.

Religion

Believing where we cannot prove.
> —Tennyson, *In Memoriam*

Between couples from the same country, different religious beliefs can be a cause of conflict in marriage, not only because the partners may not be in agreement on where and how to worship as a family, but because so much of what people do and believe, their attitudes about what is right and wrong, and their philosophy of life stem from their religious backgrounds.

In any marriage problems can arise when religious beliefs differ or when one partner's behavior conflicts with the other's beliefs. Mutual respect for each other's religion is a must for a compatible marriage, but often it is not enough. "Live and let live" doesn't work for everyone.

Some religions deny the validity of all others and insist on conversion or demand that the children be brought up in that religion. Judaism, for example, teaches that the family must repudiate (sit *shive* for) a child who marries a non-Jew; Islam demands obedience to God's law only as revealed by Mohammed. Catholics until recent years insisted that a non-Catholic partner sign a prenuptial agreement to raise any children Catholic.

In an intercultural marriage, difference in religion may be an all-inclusive issue because often an entire country runs according to the dictates of its religion or is influenced by the one which is dominant. It is frequently difficult to know where religion ends and cultural values begin.

In Muslim countries it is religion which determines the degree of freedom women have and regulates such things as gambling, dancing, sexual behavior and the use of alcohol. In Latin countries the Catholic Church, with its veneration of the Virgin Mary, is behind many of the prevailing attitudes toward women, judging them according to their approximation to her as virgins and mothers. In India the Hindu way of life, with its division of people into castes and its concept of *dharma* (system of conduct), regulates behavior. In the United States, where there are numerous religions, much of what is considered proper behavior stems from Puritan-Protestant origins.

For those couples who decide to override the dictates of their religions and marry outside them (often in the face of parental or community interference or withdrawal of support) one of three things usually happens: (1) one partner converts to the religion of the other; (2) both partners keep their own faiths and try not to interfere in the practices or beliefs of the other; or (3) both partners drift away from their own religions and either join a third religion or refrain from adhering to any formal religion at all.

Adela, a nonpracticing Cuban Catholic, was fascinated by Mohammed's Muslim faith, and, because of its rigidity, thought it would be easier for everyone if she converted to it. There were many things she had difficulty accepting, but, under Mohammed's tutelage, she tried her best to conform to the laws of the Prophet.

On the other hand, Kimberly, a self-styled American super-Jew and her Cambodian Buddhist husband, Louis, both felt strongly about their own religion and chose a system of noninterference in each other's beliefs. However, they found that they both actively practiced their faith less and regretted not being able to share it with each other.

Massimo and Tove were without strong bonds to their own religions. Many couples like Massimo and Tove raise their children without any formal religion whatsoever. Since the two found all religions equal and interesting, when they felt the need for collective prayer, they would go to the church, mosque or temple of the country to which they were currently assigned. When they were in Italy with Massimo's Catholic family, they would go to Mass with them, and when in Denmark, they would keep Tove's parents happy by attending Lutheran services.

But this kind of solution is not possible for everyone because, to many people, the form of their relationship to God is an all-important matter. One Indian Hindu, who turned his back on his faith and family to marry a Christian foreigner, was never able to make peace with his own conscience and for most of their lives together he was subject to nervous disorders, which he blamed on his religious and cultural desertion. He not only suffered feelings of guilt for his decision, but also, later on in their marriage, he developed a resentment toward the woman who had influenced his choice.

Most couples confront the religious issue before they marry and reach some sort of compromise or agreement. As regards the formal practice of religion, this arrangement often works. But religious beliefs resurface in many forms and frequently determine how a couple's life together will be played out. They affect many of the sexual practices of the couple (how many children they will have, their use of contraceptives, attitude toward abortion, fidelity, divorce); they influence how holidays will be spent (how much time will be devoted to religious ceremonies and celebrations); they often determine the food which will be served in the house, how one or both of them will dress or behave in various circumstances, their moral codes, medical practices, and so on.

Adela found that converting to Islam was not a simple matter of changing her place of worship; it meant, especially as a woman, accepting a totally different style of life. Her Iranian husband, Mohammed, not only abhorred what he considered overt sexuality on television, he expected her to repudiate it as well and to stop watching some of her favorite programs because they contained immoral scenes. She had to change her way of dressing, which meant always wearing clothes with sleeves, and give up days at the beach so dear to her Cuban heart because he could not permit his wife to be seen scantily clad by other men. She had to restrain her natural exuberance with old friends, offering the men a staid handshake in place of a friendly hug, causing her friends to wonder why she had turned so cold.

Louis and Kimberly found that their marriage was enriched by the double philosophy and traditions of their respective religions and in the beginning took turns participating in one another's ceremonies with solemn respect. All went well except for one minor problem: Louis hated Jewish food—gefilte fish, chopped liver and lox. Every Jewish holiday was a torture for him, and he began to boycott holidays with her family, thus causing arguments with his wife and hard feelings between him and his in-laws.

Couples with the same religion, but who come from different lands, often find differences in their interpretation of the doctrines and laws of their faith. Latin and Irish Catholics, for example, see things like church attendance and immorality differently; the former emphasizes the loving church and the other, the authoritarian one. Mario and Deirdre found, for example, that while both believed the same sins were sinful, one felt guiltier than the other about committing them. Sometimes partners of the same religion not only disagree but are shocked by the other's interpretation of the religious laws. Iranian and Egyptian Muslims see things quite differently, as do many American and Israeli Jews. Many African Christians combine Christianity with tribal beliefs, practices and rituals.

Even when agreements have been made and religious compromises worked out, as circumstances change these accords may no longer function and have to be reworked.

Yvette found that when she and Ali moved to Kuwait, their agreement to "live and let live" was assaulted from all sides. He was under pressure from his family to force her to convert, or at least to conform; she felt trapped and detested the restrictions placed on her by the society at large.

When children arrive, buried beliefs resurface. Sometimes adults who had stopped practicing their religions return to the fold as parents, feeling the need to impart beliefs or moralities to their offspring. Even if a couple has decided beforehand on the child's religion, one partner may only give lip service to the decision or may boycott it in subtle (or obvious) ways, showing through actions a lack of adherence to the other's teachings. Deirdre, for example, complained, "It is hard to instill religious beliefs or values all alone when the child sees the other parent doing otherwise. Inevitably the child will choose the easier route."

Many intercultural couples have thanked God that they have the bond of a common religion to help them overcome problems their other differences have caused. Others feel that a common religion is not so important as the strength of their inner beliefs and personal moral codes: it is the degree of their devoutness or spirituality which matters, whatever their religious affiliations.

Raising Children

I try to discourage mixed marriages...[but] they'll be okay as long as they can stay sterile. Once they have children, they have a problem.
> —Rabbi Stanley Rabinowitz, quoted by Janet Wallach,
> *Washington Post Magazine*, November 11, 1984

"We were fine until the children came along," is a familiar refrain of intercultural couples. Even when everything else is smooth sailing, disagreements over how best to raise the children often make the going rough. Raising children is an important issue for each parent, and each is genuinely concerned that the best thing possible be done for the children. Unfortunately (in most cases), what each sees as best is what each one has known, and even if not considered best, past experience is what will generally be repeated. People revert to their childhood to find a model for parenting, and when their upbringings took place in different countries and cultures, the models may not only be different, but conflicting.

Parents who clash over child-rearing issues are often really battling over some basic differences in philosophy, values or beliefs which they have not managed to resolve, and the child merely provides the battleground, the spark for conflict. But these issues are often difficult to define, let alone come to grips with; so, instead of going to the heart of the matter, the couple fight over the details.

Often differences show up before the child is born. What religion should he/she have? What language should be taught? Choosing the name can be a cause of discord: should it be a family name and, if so, whose family? Should the name be typical of one culture, one country, one religion, or should it be one which is acceptable to both? Should the child be raised monocultural or bicultural, monolingual or bilingual? Are the parents prepared, especially in a dual-race marriage, for the fact that the child may be a blend and not look like either parent?

There are different ideas about how infants should be handled. Should the baby sleep on its stomach or on a pile of pillows, with a wool or cotton undershirt, in a room with closed or open windows, alone or with the parents? Should it be breast- or bottle-fed, on schedule or on demand? Should its every cry be answered or should it be trained to control itself? Should it be allowed to crawl on the floor, walk barefoot, stumble and fall, or be pampered and protected from potential dangers before they present themselves? Should child care be the exclusive domain of the mother, shared by both parents, or relegated to a nursemaid or a gaggle of relatives? Should a doctor be called at every variation of temperature, and so on?

In childhood there are problems of schooling and training. Should boys and girls be educated equally? Should first sons be given preferential treatment? Is aggressiveness between siblings a preparation for the struggle ahead in life or an antisocial act? Is rebelliousness a sign of disrespect towards elders or a healthy progression toward independence? Should the schooling be done in one or both languages, one or both cultural systems? Should parents be actively involved in the child's schoolwork or should the child be responsible for his/her own work and the consequences of not doing it well? Does performing poorly at school bring shame on the entire family or on the child alone?

In early adulthood there are questions regarding how much and when to let go of the child, questions regarding sexuality, freedom and filial duty and respect. Should a girl go out alone? Should children choose their own friends, their own mates, live on their own as young adults or with their parents until they marry? The answers to these questions depend a great deal on the cultures involved.

As if it is not enough for the parents themselves to have to come to some agreement regarding these matters, the extended families (the new grandparents, uncles, aunts) often take an active role and offer advice, comments and criticism (solicited or not), and sometimes actually interfere, which makes the parents' job even harder.

Most of the arguments mentioned above arise over details, but the details are usually only surface manifestations of deeply held philosophies, values and traditions. For the sake of simplicity, we can classify most of the issues into one of three categories: (1) values and beliefs, (2) educational or disciplinary styles, and (3) forms of relationship between parent and child.

Values and beliefs, as we discussed earlier, define who we are, what is true, what is right and wrong: the "musts" and "must nots." Values and beliefs are first learned at home and are often out of our conscious awareness. Many fortunate couples discover that, despite their many other differences, their basic beliefs and values are the same, and they are able, each in his or her own way, to instill the same strong personal codes into their children. Other couples clash. When the parents' values are not only different, but conflicting, there is bound to be trouble for both parents and children.

Children whose parents are involved in a values tug-of-war may choose the value system of the more lenient parent; others will be forced to choose that of the more dominant one; others as adults will renounce both and find their own by trial and error. Still others remain confused or unsure for life.

Jaime and Cassie fought frequently over their daughter. Many of their unresolved conflicts stemmed from differences in values and came into play when there were decisions to be made regarding Jennifer. As a baby, should she be allowed to stay on the beach without any clothes; as a child, to dress in faded jeans versus freshly ironed dresses; as a teen, to choose her own friends and dates? The arguments were endless; they bickered at every stage of her growth over what appeared to be mere details, but details which reflected their culturally different ideas regarding the male-female role, virtue and good manners, etc.

The child waited each time to see who would win. She waited in vain to receive one absolute and permanent answer which would tell her what was right and what was wrong. She felt torn apart by her parents' differences, was unable to obey one without turning against the other, and finally learned to play one against the other to achieve her own goals. As time went on, Jennifer became confused and unsure of herself, and, at the same time, rebellious against any and all authority. With each battle Cassie and Jaime grew further apart. They blamed each other for everything that went wrong with the child but never faced the fact that it was their unresolved value conflicts which were causing their child-rearing disagreements.

Frequently couples claim the same values, but define them differently. Fiamma the flamboyant Italian and her English husband Andrew both taught their children to be honest, but their culturally guided interpretations of "dishonest" were different. Paying bribes and avoiding taxes were a way of life for Fiamma, but for Andrew they were forms of cheating. While both claimed the same value, their children heard a conflicting message.

Culturally different values do not always mean conflicting values, and many children of bicultural parents have benefited from the double exposure. Massimo's wife, Tove (one of whose parents had been Danish and the other Egyptian), described herself as diluted because of her two cultures and felt that she was more tolerant, more broad-minded than most of her contemporaries. "I learned at an early age to listen to two sides of every question and to think things through, not just automatically accept what I was told. As a result I believe I am more open and flexible to new ideas, new ways, different beliefs. But then again I am also strongly attached to none: maybe that's good, maybe not."

The *educational or disciplinary styles* of parents depend a great deal on their value systems: on how they perceive their roles in life, their relations with others, their perceptions of the world and themselves. In other words, how they will instruct their children to behave will depend on whether they are *doers* or *be-ers*, on whether they believe in the equality of all or in a hierarchical system, on whether they believe the world is something to be tamed for their own purposes or respected and conserved; and on whether they see themselves as individuals with their own futures to carve out, or as an integral part of a group.

With the intercultural couple, as we have seen, these value systems are sometimes the same, sometimes not—which also means that sometimes their educational methods are the same and sometimes not.

Some (Latin, Asian, Middle Eastern and many European) cultures adhere to more authoritarian methods based on patriarchal systems, while other (North American, Anglo, Scandinavian and many island) cultures are generally more lenient and permissive. This usually means that in the authoritarian family, the parental word is final and there is little room for negotiation. The child must obey. In the permissive family, children are encouraged to participate in the decision making, expressing opinions and ideas, and at least making an attempt to negotiate with the parents. These two orientations make for very different family dynamics and can be the cause of intense conflict when couples come from opposite sides of the fence.

The most frequent child-related problems encountered in these marriages revolve around differences regarding punishment of the errant child, specifically the kinds of punishment and the amount.

Yvette, for example, had no problem with Ali's authoritarian orientation, as her own upbringing had been a strict, patriarchal one, but she put her foot down at the harsh physical punishment Ali considered right and necessary to enforce his authority. Quick-tempered, he demanded unquestioning obedience and responded to any lack of it with his hands, pulling the children into submission by their hair, slapping any rebelliousness out of them and, on one or two unforgettable occasions, kicking them into silence. Not a cruel man, he merely practiced what he was used to, what he believed was the best way to teach them proper behavior. But it was treatment Yvette could not bear to witness in silence as the other women of his culture did; inevitably she interfered, only increasing his anger and, in the long run, causing him to do more physical harm to the children. As they grew older they pleaded with her not to interfere: "It only makes him get worse," they begged her.

This disagreement caused more conflict than anything else in their marriage. Ali maintained that Yvette was undermining his authority and that their children would be the worse for it; she felt she had to compensate for his undue severity by being more lenient with them than she, by nature, would have chosen to be.

Kimberly and Louis had a similar problem. He was dismayed that she yelled at and boxed their children's ears, although he knew that she was as quick to hug as to hit. Still, for him it was too physical, too loud, and too emotional. In protest he would leave the house during these scenes, causing her to claim that he wasn't helping.

Louis, however, believed in disciplining the children by withholding his love when he did not believe they merited it, which Kimberly found cold and psychologically damaging. He was especially severe with them when he felt they were being disrespectful by answering back or arguing against his decisions, or when one of them (especially one of his sons) would shame him by crying in response to punishment, while to Kimberly all of this was just healthy acting out. They never did agree, and both continued to handle the children in their own ways.

Frequently, differences in attitude toward child discipline will affect not only how the children are handled at home, but how their schooling is approached.

Lynn and Hans, who managed to hone out a pattern of life for themselves despite their differences, waged a standing battle over the education of their son Heinrich. Lynn, as a good American mother, not only was more lenient in her disciplinary methods, but believed that "learning should be fun" and resented the "parroting" method her son was being exposed to in the Austrian schools. She fought against it: she fought the teachers, she fought the system, and she fought with her husband while Heinrich awaited the outcome. Hans maintained that the American way left children without *durrchalten*, or backbone, without a sense of the value of hard work and endurance, as well as lacking in the automatic respect for authority figures which he considered essential to a child's formation. The teachers complained that Heinrich did not have the proper family support to be a good student (a mother who did his homework with him). Heinrich, caught in the middle, struggled to do his best amidst the confusion.

Cecil and Ikumi had differences of opinion regarding child upbringing typical of East-West marriages—to which was added Cecil's adherence to the British belief in the benefits of boarding school. Although she recognized that sending their son back to England to be educated was better in some ways, considering the nomadic life they led in the foreign service, she never fully forgave him for insisting on doing so when the boy was only ten years of age.

Hiroshi and Dorrie had many similar problems. Dorrie objected to the Japanese school system as being "stifling" while Hiroshi pointed to the superior scholastic results. Dorrie strongly opposed the prevalent use of corporal punishment while Hiroshi defended the rights of the teachers. "Truthfully," Dorrie confessed, "I have a problem with the whole system of raising and educating children in Japan. Hiroshi's idea of what my role as a mother should be is in total contrast with my own. I didn't believe that I should sleep with the newborn while my husband got his rest down the hall, nor did I go along with breast feeding until the child was two years old. It all goes with the Japanese view that the child is an extension of the mother. I see us as independent beings which is alien and wrong to him."

In most of these cases the parents' differences appear to have done little damage. The children adapted effectively, learning what to expect and just how far they could go with each parent, which in a way prepared them at an early age for dealing with different kinds of people in their lives.

These disciplinary methods, and the kind of family style which they represent—authoritarian or permissive—strongly affect *parent-child relationships*. The authoritarian family runs on a "rules over feelings" doctrine and the atmosphere is formal and respectful. The houses are set up to enforce this atmosphere, with parlors for adults only and formal dining rooms where Papa presides and the children watch their manners and curb their tongues.

The permissive type of family is usually more casual, spontaneous, nurturing, and more concerned with expressing feelings than applying rules; it uses feedback, and explains the reasons behind decisions. Houses usually reflect this style, revolving around the family room, which is everyone's domain. [23]

When styles of interfamily relating are culturally different, couples usually choose one of three courses. They may follow the customs of the land. This usually means that the expatriate spouse gives in to the other's style. In some ways this is the easiest on the child because there is consistency between how people act with one another, both in and outside the home. Helga, for example, submerged herself in her husband's Libyan culture, speaking his language and adopting his manners, including the way in which she related to their children. She felt that presenting a united front would serve the children as role models in their future relationships with others. But this method, while advantageous in certain respects, involves a certain negation of self on the part of the foreign partner. When Helga moved alone with them to Geneva, she reverted to her own German-style family relating, leaving the children perplexed over the inconsistency.

The second possibility is to adopt the style of one partner: often that of the more dominant one, or of the man in male-dominant cultures; sometimes the style of the woman when

---

[23] For more information on this subject, read "Out of House and Home," in Condon and Yousef, *An Introduction to Intercultural Communication*, pp 147-67.

child-rearing is considered her exclusive domain, regardless of where they are living.

In some cases allowing one parent to dominate works; in others it can be disastrous. For example, Adela submitted to her husband's will and allowed him to create a strictly Muslim home, but their children were exposed to totally different and appealing alternate lifestyles in the Philadephia public schools they attended. In their case the conflict of lifestyles became too much for their youngest daughter, Jasmine, who fled from home at age sixteen to escape the ambivalence of her life—a father who was so different from the people around them and a mother whom she saw as too weak to fight him.

Milee and Harry educated their children in the Australian manner, sent them to local schools where they spoke English, played Australian sports and joined in a variety of extracurricular activities. However, when they entered their home, the children were expected by their mother and Vietnamese resident relatives to become perfect Asian children, deferring to their parents' wishes without argument, eating her food and controlling any Western impulses they may have picked up on the outside. Harry had some trouble with this pattern but was outnumbered because of the constant presence of Milee's family and because he was away too much on assignments around the country to exert much influence.

The third alternative is for both parents to behave individually in their own naturally comfortable way with their children. This usually happens when both partners are from fairly egalitarian cultures, when both are considered equal partners in the marriage and when each respects the other. This was the case with Massimo and Tove because both partners liked and admired the other's culture, felt that each parent had something special to offer, and did not interfere with how each worked out his/her personal relationship with the children.

The primary disadvantage for children of these parents, who each relate to them in different ways, is that they often have no clear-cut example of how to relate to their peers or to other adults. These children may become withdrawn or shy because they don't have a clear and instinctive sense of how to behave.

Other bicultural children benefit from the double example; they learn at an early age how to get along with all kinds of people and become effective communicators who are more alert to signals and nonverbal messages than others. They can sense more quickly what different people expect; they can use their cross-cultural skills and become true international citizens.

Raising children is the real test of how well a couple has learned to handle their many differences because with children all the issues surface and must be confronted. Successful intercultural parents are generally successful intercultural spouses.

Language/Communication

I tried to say I love you, but the words got in the way.
—*Miami Sound Machine,* Epic Records (CBS, Inc.)

At the beginning of their relationship, each partner in an intercultural couple tends to take for granted that his/her way of communicating is universal, obvious, clear and right—and assumes that the other has understood. "And in interpreting what others say, we assume they mean what we would mean if we said the same thing in the same way."[24] Only later do they begin to see that that is not true and they begin to wonder whether they understand each other at all.

Communication is sharing meaning and includes everything we use to exchange meaning with one another: words, tone of voice, a shoulder shrug, a yawn. It is hard enough for us in our own languages to express our thoughts and feelings, to be understood, and to be sure we really understand others. When we try to communicate with a spouse (perhaps in his or her

[24] Deborah Tannen, *That's Not What I Meant,* p 27.

language) from a different linguistic and cultural background (as well as of the opposite sex), it is that much harder. Good communication is perhaps the most essential ingredient in a successful marriage, and it is probably the most difficult thing to achieve in an intercultural one. How a couple shares meaning pretty much determines the kind of relationship they will have.

Researchers have found that the "average person spends 50% to 80% of his day listening, but hears only half of what is said, understands only a quarter of that, and remembers even less."[25] In our own language we tune out, half listen, become distracted, or are busy preparing our answers instead of really hearing. If listening is inherently such a difficult task, it is no wonder that intercultural couples have such a struggle with it.

Man Keung Ho, in his book *Building a Successful Intermarriage*,[26] makes use of the Chinese word *ting* (listen) to explain its complexity. *Ting* is a composite of four vital parts.

[25] Don Oldenberg, "In One Ear...," *Washington Post*, 2/27/87, Style Plus section, p C5.
[26] Man Keung Ho, *Building a Successful Intermarriage*, p 98.

The ear is necessary for hearing the words spoken, the eye for seeing the message conveyed by the body, the mind for interpreting the meaning of what has been seen and heard, and the heart for being able to feel what is wanted and needed from the relationship.[27]

In order for intercultural couples to overcome their communication handicaps they have to work harder at listening, using the heart and mind as well as the eye and ear to avoid misunderstandings.

Other obstacles block communication also. Usually one of the two is not speaking his or her own language, which means that the message is possibly distorted by the accent or misuse of words by the foreign speaker and possibly only partially understood by the listener. Then the message sent and received is subject to each listener's interpretation, which depends on his/her own personal and cultural frame of reference (including such things as expectations, insecurities, wants, values, beliefs, prejudices). With such stumbling blocks, it's a wonder anything is communicated at all! But it is; it just takes a lot of hard work and patience.

In trying to unravel some of the mysteries of communication, it may help to examine its three major components—verbal, nonverbal, and stylistic. All three together can cause major problems for two people who do not come from the same linguistic and cultural background but who are trying to achieve an intimate relationship. Sometimes it takes years of practice and delving into hidden meanings for these couples to learn how to communicate with each other. Some of them never really learn.

Verbal communication refers to the words we speak and transmits the sense of what we want to say. At best, however, words are imperfect communicators, and for people who don't have the same mother tongue they can be dangerous. It is not always easy in another language to know what words should be used when or to whom. Different rules apply in different cultures, and the wrong or inappropriate word can bring about

[27] *Ibid*, p 98.

misunderstandings. A harmless expletive in one language, translated literally into another, can be shocking or wounding; a "you" instead of a "thou" in some languages (French and German) can imply a familiarity which is not intended or proper.

All languages are made up of idiomatic phrases, shortcut labels, and titles which convey certain meanings without elaborating. But these can be dangerous when conversing with someone with a different mother tongue.

Titles, for example, are basically job descriptions—they describe the person who does this or that. But as many couples have found, certain titles carry different cultural interpretations. "Mother" to Rosemary, for example, was the nurturer who led her children into adulthood and then let them go. To her Indian mother-in-law, however, "Mother" was the eternal presence in the lives of her children, dictating their lifestyles and demanding overt demonstrations of their loyalty. Ravi was caught in the middle, trying to find a meaning which satisfied both his own mother and the mother of his children.

In addition to the words themselves, language often affects the balance of power in an intercultural marriage. Generally one partner is speaking his own language and the other is not (except where both speak the same language or a third language); and as language is power, the more fluent partner has the upper hand and automatically takes the lead. Superior linguistic facility, speed, and vocabulary can not only direct the conversation and set its style, but can also manipulate it to serve personal ends. This is where the balance in the relationship shifts, with the fluent one having the advantage; and whenever things are unbalanced, the relationship suffers.

Jaime, because of his limited knowledge of English, had to lean on Cassie for many things which he considered his male prerogative, and he resented it. Cassie, in turn, became impatient with Jaime's ineffectuality. She got tired of having to do everything "because no one else understands him," and despite herself, often became critical and bossy, which neither of them liked.

At the same time, Cassie made no attempt to learn Spanish. Something inside her prevented her: basically, she liked having the upper hand in this one important area. She liked the power that speaking in her own language gave her over a husband whose traditions taught him that women were slightly inferior beings. It was a small thing, but she hung onto it.

Both Cassie and Jaime commented on the fact that not having the same native language created tension in their daily lives, a tension which was draining. "Often we found that this tension spread over and caused arguments which shouldn't have happened, which had nothing to do with the topic at the time. Because of the difficulties of communication, neither of us was relaxed; both of us were like time bombs waiting to go off."

Lynn felt so strongly about not wanting to be helpless and dependent that she made a concerted effort to learn to speak and read German. In fact, she ended up speaking it better than Hans spoke English, and so it became their language. But her sense of accomplishment waned when she had a difficult concept to explain, a deep feeling to express, or a point of view to defend, and the words just didn't come out right. She would splutter hopelessly while Hans won out (right or wrong) through sheer verbal agility. Out of frustration she found that she often lashed out at him "like a viper," to compensate for her inadequacy with language.

Lynn also commented that she had "lost [her] personality in the translation, as well as [her] sense of humor." She felt she was leading a kind of double life: one personality in one language, another in the other...kind of an intercultural schizophrenic." As she put it: "In English I am a funny, clever woman; in German, I become a *Dummkopf*. In fact the more I speak in German, the more I think I really am becoming dull. I miss the intellectual stimulation of conversing with people at the same level and in my own language, the repartee I had back home. We both have to watch so carefully not to misunderstand one another that it takes much of the fun out of talking."

It is often claimed that humor is the most difficult aspect of learning a language. Neither the words nor the concepts translate very well. Different cultures think different things are funny and make use of humor and wit in their own ways.

Deirdre made use of wit when things "became so totally

impossible that there was nothing else to do but laugh." She was also able to laugh at her own weaknesses and mistakes. Mario thought she needed to "have her head examined" to see how she could laugh "when she should have been crying." He also found her wit caustic, not funny. What he didn't understand was that laughing or making a joke was her way of overcoming a desperate situation. She, in turn, thought that if he could forget *bella figura* and learn to take himself a little less seriously, it would be better for both of them.

Milee, on the other hand, often felt like crying—tears of frustration—because she was never able to see what was funny about Harry's jokes. His Australian friends thought he was very funny and wondered how he could have married someone with no sense of humor. But she knew how to laugh (she loved the American comedian Peewee Herman, for example, and decided his was "Vietnamese humor" which Harry never did catch on to). She simply didn't understand her husband's jokes, even when they were painstakingly explained to her.

"I thought he was crazy," she said. "I thought they all were crazy. Then I tried laughing when the others were laughing but found that I was laughing at the wrong things and shocking everyone. Only Harry knew that I didn't understand, but when he explained to the others that I didn't know what I was laughing at, I felt even more ashamed and stupid. So we just gave up."

Communication depends also on signals which the speaker gives (and the listener receives and interprets in his or her own way) through unspoken body language or *nonverbal communication.*

Just as the spoken language usually differs for couples from different cultural backgrounds, the nonverbal or body language is likely to be dissimilar as well. Whenever people talk, *all* of them is talking. Each of us makes use of a large set of nonverbal signals which convey meaning, sometimes more than the words themselves: tone of voice, intonations, facial gestures (grimaces, arched eyebrows, half-smiles, frowns), eye contact (either looking or not looking into another's eyes), body movements (drumming fingers, shrugging shoulders, waving arms), posture (slouched or poised erectly), breathing patterns and the distance maintained between speakers (intimately close or formally distant). These things together form the framework for our spoken words and help send our message, and these visible signals are interpreted differently from culture to culture.

Many people are aware that the nonverbal aspect of a language really determines their fluency because this visible expressiveness often conveys information that is crucial to the understanding of the message. Unfortunately, it is difficult to learn because most nonverbal language is out of the awareness of the speakers.

In some cultures people gesture more than in others. Similar gestures may have different meanings; faces may be inscrutable or openly emotional; some languages may sound loud or harsh; some people talk all the time, while others make use of silence to transmit messages. Some cultures take the direct approach to convey meaning, while others are masters of innuendo and subtlety. Arabs, for example, depend on eye contact to build trust, while Japanese feel that too much eye contact is intrusive and rude.

Milee, for example, gave the impression of being shy and passive because she kept her eyes lowered when talking. Harry felt helpless: "Look at me so I can see what you are saying," he would say. She tried, but it was awkward for her.

One of the most frustrating things about nonverbal language is that you can't run to the dictionary to determine the meanings. Often, it can only be learned by trial and error. Some things can be explained. When people do something wrong or rude in another country (such as crossing legs and showing the sole of the foot in Muslim lands), it may be pointed out to them; they learn not to repeat the offense. But other nonverbal signals are intangible—although not actually wrong, they send out messages which were not intended and are harder to recognize and correct. For this reason intercultural couples have to be doubly aware of each other's nonverbal communication and must be careful that their own is being correctly understood.

Mario did not see that his standing six inches away from

Deirdre, with tensed shoulders and piercing eyes, while he shouted put Deirdre off before she heard his first words; these things were natural to him. He did not understand that her sharp retort was her natural defensive reaction to what she thought was the beginning of a fight...which then became a fight when Mario, in turn, reacted to her reaction. Each blamed the other for starting the fight, which neither of them wanted; but they were in a vicious circle of miscommunication which, of course, got worse instead of better. Innocent conversations escalated into conflict, which was born less of different ideas and beliefs than of different ways of expressing them.

Yvette and Ali, on the other hand, because their cultures were so far apart (French/Kuwaiti) and both spoke a language (English) which was native to neither of them, were used to not automatically understanding each other and took time to ask for explanations and to describe to each other how the other's behavior made them feel. Ali was able to tell Yvette that her use of makeup, her style of dressing and her French perfume embarrassed him when they were in his country because it gave a message to others which he knew she did not intend. She was able to tell him that his habit "of practically sitting on someone" when he was talking to them was too close for comfort for most Europeans. They didn't necessarily agree with each other, but they usually managed to get their points across—carefully, tactfully, and painstakingly—never assuming, always reconfirming: "I hear you saying.... Is that what you want to say?" But they managed (not without occasional difficulties) because they were each aware of their differences and took the time to clarify.

Styles of conversing are also different for different people. By styles we mean people's manner of carrying on a conversation, their patterns of behaving and relating to others. There are no right or wrong styles, simply different styles. They often depend on the individual's age, education and sex. Women, for example, are "often more attuned than men to the meta-messages of talk...[they] are more likely to be indirect, and to try to reach agreement by negotiation...[and] often end up appearing deferential and unsure of themselves or of what they want."[28] "Also men expect to *do* things together and don't feel anything is missing if they don't have heart-to-heart talks all the time."[29]

Styles also vary significantly across cultures. Some cultures are direct, while others have elaborate systems of linguistic courtesy; some make extensive use of irony and figures of speech; some engage in elegant forms of greeting and salutations; some believe less in the value of the spoken word as a means of expressing thoughts and feelings than do others; some do not always say what they mean, and others do not always mean what they say.

Mario's style was by turns bombastic, demonstrative, frank, direct, fast, probing and aggressive. Deirdre's was in contrast subtle, distant, tentative, discreet, cutting, and conciliatory. Harry's was ponderous, personal and friendly (informal), full of exaggerations, word plays, humor, and slang. Milee's in contrast was reserved, indirect, and detached (formal). She believed in silences whereas he couldn't bear them. She felt some things were better left unsaid, while he couldn't understand what he couldn't hear. It was hard for her to say aloud, "I love you," for example, or "I don't want...," but for Harry she tried to learn.

Couples who have culturally different styles of communicating feel they are on different levels, "talking to the wind" or passing right by each other. They may also believe that the other is simply not polite because their assumptions of what constitutes good manners differ. As Andy Capp, the British cartoon character, put it, "Culture to that lass is practically anything her crowd does and my crowd doesn't."[30]

The truth is that different styles apply to different peoples, and true communication between intercultural couples requires that they learn to understand, accept, and accommodate each other's style, as well as learn to cope with the complications which arise from the differences in both their verbal and nonverbal languages. It takes a lot of work, but the results of the effort are well worth the investment.

[28] Deborah Tannen, pp 126-27.
[29] *Ibid*, p 98.
[30] Reggie Smythe, cartoon in *Washington Post*, 4/24/87.

Dealing with Stress

...there are, however, variations, not only in customs but also in drives and feelings.
—Karen Horney,*The Neurotic Personality of Our Time*

Just as differences in communication can be a big hurdle in intercultural marriages, so too can culturally different ways of handling stress and/or resolving conflict.

Stress, which is anything pushing us mentally or physically out of kilter, can be caused by external, accidental situations such as death, sickness, loss of job, problems with a child, or even a marital fight. Change—the birth of a child, moves, new jobs, retirement—can also cause stress. The causes of stress may not be of themselves momentous, but may be an accumulation of small crises which cause an overload. Sometimes stress is caused by the difficulties in dealing with the marital situation itself, in learning to live with another person, especially if the partners approach life and how to live it from very different viewpoints. Whatever the cause, each of us has ways of meeting stress, depending on our age, sex, personality and cultural or ethnic background.

Monocultural couples also have to face stress-related problems, but when the ethnic backgrounds are different, the spouses frequently don't know where to begin looking for solutions. The ways people react to stress are generally unconscious and so are especially hard to identify and/or alter.

We receive our first lessons on how to cope with life in our own homes, from our parents, from schools, and from peers. Much depends on the kinds of experiences we have on our way to adulthood and how we are taught to react to them. In some cultures, for example, a child learns that it is all right, even healthy, to cry, while in others, crying is shameful or a sign of weakness. One culture may encourage displays of righteous anger, while another teaches self-control. One instructs people to fight for what they want; another believes in passive acceptance of what life brings.

When two people are from the same culture, they can usually at least comprehend (if not fully agree with or share) each other's way of handling such things as sadness, anger, grief, worry, conflict, illness, or death, and usually know what kind of response is expected. But when they are not from the same or similar backgrounds, they may be not only puzzled, but upset by each other's behavior, and react accordingly.

Karen Horney says, "Every culture clings to the belief that its own feelings and drives are the one normal expression of human nature."[31] We judge ourselves (and others) according to our approximation to what our society considers normal. When these norms differ, it is hard to know what to think, how to judge, or how to react to another's behavior.

This can be a problem for intercultural couples. One partner may not understand what is going on with the other, may interpret the other's behavior incorrectly, and react in a negative or inappropriate way (which in turn may be misinterpreted), until the whole situation catapults out of control.

"...couples often react to each other as though the other's behavior were a personal attack rather than just a difference rooted in ethnicity. Typically, we tolerate differences when we are not under stress. In fact, we find them appealing. However, when stress is added to a system, our tolerance for difference diminishes. We become frustrated if we are not understood in ways that fit our wishes and expectations."[32]

Kimberly was brought up in a Jewish-American family, where everyone thrived on "letting it all out" and on analyzing every situation ad infinitum. She was, in her words, "nearly driven mad" by her Cambodian husband Louis, who wouldn't tell what he was thinking or feeling when he was obviously troubled, but would silently contemplate his fish tanks, oblivious

---

[31] Karen Horney, *Neurotic Personality of Our Times*, p 16.
[32] McGoldrick, Pearce and Giordano, *Ethnicity and Family Therapy*, pp 21-22.

of her attempts to find out what was wrong. He needed to be left alone, to work things out in quiet and solitude. He not only didn't share Kimberly's tactics, but was agonized by her tears and her emotions. He felt that talking about them cheapened them.

Mario and Deirdre stockpiled resentments and wounds born of their conflicting Latin and Irish-American ways of handling stress. Each new incident brought back past incidents and triggered reactions resulting from years of misunderstanding and intolerance. Even though they had learned to understand one another's coping strategies, they rejected them as unacceptable.

Victor, who was accustomed in his precise Swiss-German way of accepting pain and grief with silent dignity, was shaken and disdainful of his Tunisian wife Zehyra's histrionics whenever something went wrong. He began to dismiss real problems as one more case of Middle Eastern dramatics. When her father died, Zehyra's tearful wailing seemed exaggerated to him, almost insincere. Although he knew her grief was real, her way of expressing it put him off because it was so unlike what he considered a proper display of emotion. He tried to help her get control of herself, which was not at all what she wanted or needed at the moment. She saw his reaction as a confirmation of what she felt was his essential coldness and lack of feeling.

The problem is that, although whatever works for the individual is valid, marital partners have to cooperate to resolve many problems—which means that they have to first learn how to interpret the other's behavior and respond appropriately to it.

Kimberly, in time, learned to slow down and to stop probing Louis with nonstop questions designed to force him to open up. In turn he learned to tell her what he wanted and needed and to let her express her feelings to him. Only then were they able to create an interactive pattern which respected the behaviors of each and provided them with alternate methods of dealing with problems. She learned to appreciate his calm persistence in moments when she was flying off the handle and he to kick up his heels once in a while and become more open and spontaneous. Neither really changed, but both rounded the rough edges and found ways of coping with the other's way of coping.

This doesn't always work because when people are under stress, they are not at their best, and while some coping styles can be complementary, others are conflicting. However, if the partners constantly challenge each other's methods, one or both of them may begin to lose trust in the other, then to have self-doubts, and to lose a degree of the self-assurance which allows them to be themselves around the other.

Illness and Suffering

To each his suff'rings: all are men.
—Thomas Gray, *In a Distant Prospect of Eton College*

One stress-causing matter which can be particularly difficult for intercultural couples to handle has to do with illness and suffering, which involves how each answers such questions as: How sick is sick? What is healthy? How can illness be prevented? How should it be reacted to? Who should treat it and how?

When a husband and wife come from different cultures, they may have opposing answers to these questions.

In their excellent book, *Ethnicity and Family Therapy*, McGoldrick, Pearce and Giordano[33] have stated that people differ across cultures in

1. how they experience pain;
2. what they label as a symptom;
3. how they communicate their pain or symptoms;
4. what their beliefs are about the cause of illness;
5. how they regard helpers (doctors and therapists);
6. what treatment they desire or expect.

[33] *Ibid*, pp 6-7.

The way people experience pain is influenced by culture. In some cultures, the norm or ideal is to suffer silently while in others one is expected or allowed to be more demonstrative and verbal in responding to pain.

What is labeled as a symptom also differs from culture to culture. For example, "Among women in the United States, a benign small lump in the breast is charged with fearsome cultural significance. Among the Chinese, mild dizziness is believed to heighten susceptibility to neurasthenia. The patient is overly sensitive to such symptoms, and strong reactions result. In contrast, symptoms that have meaning for health professionals, such as black stools and easy bruising, may be seen as normal or expected in areas where such symptoms are highly prevalent. Culturally informed perceptions may also lead to somatic preoccupation, complaints, illness labeling and help-seeking due to selective attention."[34]

Fiamma and Andrew were at opposite ends of the spectrum when it came to communicating their pain and symptoms. When Fiamma was expecting their first child, she complained for nine months and screamed with abandon throughout childbirth in true Italian style. Andrew, who had opted to be with her when the child was born, was torn apart by her expressions of agony and exhausted by the whole ordeal. Later he was amazed to hear her describe her child's birth. "It was nothing. Of course I screamed like a hyena through the whole thing." This was said with a shrug of her shoulders as if it were the most natural thing in the world. Andrew could remember his English mother telling his sister at the time of her birthing, "Keep your mouth shut and remember you're a lady."

Fiamma, on the other hand, never knew when Andrew was sick because of his stoic British way of keeping silent about his suffering. She was offended when he turned his back on her attempts to make a fuss over him, taking it as a personal rejection. She wondered why he was refusing her love and solicitude.

---

[34] Taken from a paper submitted by S. Kanu Dunn to the Third National Conference on the Transcultural Family, 1986.

Beliefs about the causes of illness vary according to cultural background and will often dictate how they are to be treated. According to some, illness may result from breathing the night air, while others will swear that fresh air at night prevents illness. In some cultures, people rigidly adhere to rules of cleanliness as infection preventives, while in others all the fuss about hygiene is regarded as exaggerated nonsense. Some cultural groups place stock in witchcraft, believing that illnesses are the result of a curse or spell or are a punishment for a past evil deed. Illness can be perceived as caused by one's own carelessness or inattention or by fate, over which one has no control.

Whenever Sune (the Swede) became ill, he was sure it was his own fault: he hadn't taken good enough care of his body and so cured himself by dieting and exercising. His Malaysian wife, Rani, accepted illness and pain as part of what life had in store for her. She was resigned to it and at best turned to a combination of herbs and medication to deal with it. Neither agreed with the other, but both let the other do as he/she liked.

Attitudes also vary greatly about doctors and other helpers. Some believe they are the most qualified to treat illness. In other cultures people have more faith in spiritualists, faith healers, witches, medicine men, or God.

Some couples accept each other's preferences concerning health care providers, but others insist on conformity to their own beliefs. Iranian Mohammed insisted that Adela go to a female rather than a male doctor whenever she was not well. He himself rarely went to any medical professional (it was part of his manly pride to be able to handle pain and take care of himself). Joachim took their son Jorge to the parish priest in Portugal to resolve his bouts of depression rather than permitting Canadian Sara to take him to a psychologist.

Intercultural couples can also disagree about treatment for their illnesses. Should they buy over-the-counter drugs, use cures handed down through the family or natural herbs and roots as the Chinese and others have done for centuries, or should they use no medicines whatsoever?

Old beliefs and rituals still prevail; traditional cures are used instead of, or often together with, modern medical practices. Many educated people have more faith in what family history has proven than in modern medicine. Aside from what the spouses themselves adhere to, the health conditions where they live will often have a profound effect on their lives, especially if they live in a country where medical care is difficult to obtain. Sometimes one spouse does not trust the medical practices of the partner's country or has to leave for treatment because the facilities are inadequate.

One Scottish bride, who followed her husband to Yemen, developed an incurable kidney disease which could not be treated in her husband's homeland. She was forced to go to England for the needed care, while he remained behind because he could not leave his job. They spent most of their lives separated, visiting each other once or twice a year, whenever he could afford to make the trip.

While the couples are young, healthy and without children, issues of illness often don't arise, but when children are born or when one of the partners becomes seriously ill, deep-seated feelings and beliefs about illness may surface.

Ethnocentrism

Cosi é se vi pare. **(Right you are if you think you are.)**
—Pirandello
Human beings are perhaps never more frightening than when they are convinced beyond doubt that they are right.
—Laurens Van der Post, *The Lost World of the Kalahari*

The ability to see the world as one's partner sees it, to understand life from the other's vantage point, to empathize with this other point of view, to allow for it and meet it halfway may be the true secret to making it over the other obstacles to a successful intercultural marriage.

How able the partners are to walk in the others' shoes depends on just how ethnocentric (unalterably convinced of the rightness of their own ways) they are. Webster defines *ethnocentrism* as: "the emotional attitude that one's own race, nation, or culture is superior to all others."[35]

All of us are ethnocentric to a certain degree, convinced that our way is the only (or right) way, and we judge others according to their approximation to our way. All of us need to be ethnocentric about some things: it gives us stability and consistency, and is part of what makes us what we are. But when people are ethnocentric about almost everything, it means they are intolerant and inflexible and will probably have a hard time making a relationship work, especially an intercultural relationship.

When two ethnocentric people marry, they are often unwilling to consider that there may be alternate, but equally valid ways of being and of doing things. They not only disagree or disparage each other's ways, but also try to convert them to their own. Although the more dominant one may prevail, something basic is lost, for the only way intercultural marriages can succeed is for the partners to realize that there are many ways to look at the world and to find a compromise which is reasonably satisfactory to *both* of them.

Some people are less ethnocentric by nature than others. Generally, the person who lives in the other's country is the one who has to be more open, more broad-minded. When the expatriate spouse resists adapting to the ways of the land, she or he spends a lifetime discontented with what fate has dealt, and views the local inhabitants with contempt.

Of the two, Jaime was less ethnocentric than Cassie. Although he struggled with aspects of life in the United States which went against his grain, he was at least open to trying them. Cassie, however, fought anything which was different, and they both knew she would never have adjusted to living in Santo Domingo. Although she learned to cook a few of his native

[35] Webster's *Deluxe Unabridged Dictionary*, 1983.

dishes and enjoyed most of his friends—as long as they spoke English—and went willingly with him to visit his family, she relaxed only when she was back home with her friends in her own milieu.

Sara, out of necessity, bowed to many of the ways of Portugal, but not without a degree of contempt. She never overcame her conviction that Portugal would be a better place if the people would just "join the modern world and stop eating and sleeping their days away." Nothing ever made her alter her feeling of cultural superiority, and she rarely missed a chance to point it out (which made her less than popular with many of Joachim's friends).

Traditionally, women have been more open to compromise than men, more interested in preserving the relationship; they have taken its success as their responsibility and its failure as their fault.

New York-born Lynn was convinced that the only way to make her marriage work was to embrace the country and culture of her husband (with the exception of the school system), to submerge herself in it, to stop speaking her own language (even to her own children), to cook Austrian food and to spend time with exclusively Austrian friends.

For years this seemed to work, but the time finally came when she felt she had lost something fundamental to her being, that she had betrayed her own values. Her ethnocentrism, dormant for years, reemerged and made her dissatisfied with her life. But it was almost too late for her to change the pattern; any attempts she made merely confused her husband and children, and they wondered what was wrong with her. They had assumed that his way had become her way and that everyone, including Lynn, was satisfied with the arrangement.

Some cultures are more flexible than others and tolerate alternate patterns of living. Others automatically exclude anything different. People who marry into a culture which requires conformity must be ready to embrace it totally. In Kenya there was only one way for a woman to behave. If Rashida, Olu's wife, did not live up to that way, she was bad. There was no compromise. Her ways or opinions were not valid. Similarly, Mohammed had made it clear to Adela when they decided to marry that she must conform to Islamic culture, even though they lived in the U.S. As her own background had taught her to bow to her husband's will, she agreed; but her life became a struggle, not only to live up to standards not her own, but to deal with having to repress her own needs and wants.

The ideal situation is when both partners are mature and flexible enough to remain independent and individual, able to acknowledge the other's individuality, and to accept that both have ethnocentric needs which must be respected—and possibly to recognize that sometimes the other's ways may even work better. American Kimberly and Cambodian Louis were fascinated by each other's cultures and were open enough to admit to faults within their own. They were able to overcome some of their ethnocentrism and to try new things and different ways. It gave them a creative approach to their life together. World diplomats Massimo and Tove, who admittedly were attached to very little, claimed they didn't know what ethnocentrism meant. Life together in their eyes was truly a mix, an experiment, an international cocktail which was concocted by using a "little of this, a little of that, in different ways every day—sometimes better, sometimes not, but never, ever dull...."

THE EXPATRIATE SPOUSE

Upstairs in my room I listen to Joan Baez records all day and cry. I know how the Sikkimese got their eyes—little damn Mongolian eyes; they damn well cried all the time.
—Hope Cooke, *Time Change*

The role of the expatriate spouse is not an easy one, no matter how willingly chosen or how second nature it has become, because it is always that: *second* nature, not first. The spouse who will be going to live in the other's country must think seriously about what that might mean—changing from a familiar, comfortable way of life to a new, strange one, in which almost everything has to be learned. It may mean feeling frustrated with one's own inadequacies or with the difficulties in learning to function effectively in another language, another style, according to other rules and criteria. It usually means coping with different foods, climates, medical practices, housing conditions, laws, standards of living, and political atmospheres. It always means leaving behind loved ones and supportive friends in exchange for others who will always be different and who will forever regard the foreigner as different, not quite one of them. Finally, it usually means living with a sense of isolation and confusion, of having a double identity. The partner who will become the expatriate spouse must think carefully about these considerations and have a fair idea as to whether they present challenges or obstacles, opportunities for growth or risks of failure. Also the expatriate spouse who has married into the culture and moved there with no plans, and perhaps few possibilities, of ever returning home except as a visitor will find that the pressures to acculturate are so strong that the difficulty of adjustment can be extreme.

There are various ways to handle this pressure. One can (1) refuse to adapt and choose instead to reject the partner's culture totally, continuing to think and act as if at home, (2) let oneself be submerged in the other culture and reject one's own, (3) behave one way in one culture and another way in the other, (4) blend the two cultures into a new one entirely one's own.

Those who are extremely ethnocentric or have no respect for the other's culture, carry on with their lives as though they were still at home: they live in little ghettos, associating only with people of their own country, speaking their own language, importing their clothes, and cooking and eating primarily their own food. They often force the spouse to become a foreigner in his or her own land. Of course, despite their best efforts, some of the other culture rubs off on them, but they resist it as best they can.

When Miguel moved to America, he did so to please Carol and because the opportunities for them were better there than in his native Chile. But as previously said, he never identified with the culture of his wife. He made it clear to her that if she wanted to keep him, if she loved him, she would help create a little "Chilean haven" in their home. At the same time, he suffered with the struggle and lashed out violently in confusion and frustration. He experienced frequent bouts of depression and didn't know what to do about them. For Carol, Miguel's failure to adjust was also difficult. She felt as though she were living in two countries, that her life was segmented. When she came home from work the music on the record player, the language spoken, the cooking aromas in the air, the pictures on the walls and the rugs on the floor were all distinctly Chilean; even the rules of comportment and the details of their lifestyle were unlike mainstream America. She also suffered from having to apologize to her husband for her own culture.

The spouses who try to lose themselves in the spouse's culture often disclaim their own in doing so. They become "more Roman than the Romans," eating, drinking, dressing and adhering to all the accepted modes of behavior of the other culture. Some deny their instincts, beliefs, and feelings; they give up their independent sense of self—as Lynn did.

The problem with this kind of immersion is that, in the long run, these spouses never quite become part of the other culture, they only become alienated from themselves. They are like actors who put on costumes and get so caught up in the role they are playing that they lose touch with themselves. They never fully overcome their sense of alienation; they merely add a layer which hides or disguises it. Often these expatriate spouses appear to have adjusted the best, but underneath they are suffering from the falsity of their lives. As Lynn explained it: "One day I woke up with the strangest sense of having lost myself somewhere along the way. Who am I? What do I believe in? I'd lost all sense of my own past identity and didn't know what I had become."

At the same time she became aware that the blush was off

the romance, that her marriage was no longer the exciting fairy tale she had expected it to be. She began to question the wisdom of having married Hans and given up the comfortable regularity of life in the United States, and she didn't know where to turn. She had cut herself off from her old world, from people like herself who would understand her doubts and dilemmas. Having burned her bridges, she didn't know how to go forward, and she couldn't go back. Worst of all, she wasn't sure anymore who she was.

Adela also had submerged herself in her husband's Islamic culture if not his country when she married him, losing her own in the process. She described her life as "living in a constant state of confusion, with no familiar landmarks to help one along. The things I thought I was sure about are constantly challenged in this new world I inhabit, until I begin to question them myself. I get to the point where I'm not sure any more what is right and what is wrong. I find myself doing things out of character because I think that's how they are supposed to be done. Sometimes I feel as though what is going on around me is not real, as though I were living a movie. I'm never sure what I'm supposed to do or be or what is going to happen next."

Other spouses manage to adopt what they consider best in the other culture, without rejecting or losing their own. They behave according to the demands of the situation. Sometimes they even think in two different ways to suit the circumstances. Beneath it all they know who they are and what they believe in, but they can see the value in the other point of view and the necessity for adapting their own behavior to it. But the balance is difficult to maintain and can cause considerable strain and exhaustion.

When Yvette moved with Ali to Kuwait she brought her own language, religion, clothes, and cuisine, which she maintained in their home. She studied interior design in order to "do something with myself to keep from going crazy," chosing a field which was acceptable for a woman to enter in Kuwait. As a professional interior designer she preserved a degree of her own identity, of independence and also of financial self-sufficiency, which were important to her pride and her sense of self. "It was already hard enough being like a child, learning how to cope with minor daily details, being dependent on my husband for *everything*. At least this part-time occupation helped me feel like a functioning adult."

Still, Yvette made a point of learning Arabic and she followed the customs and rules of Kuwait whenever it was appropriate for her to do so. She made sure her children learned about their father's faith and customs and adhered to them, but she remained her own person.

Nevertheless, she complained of the strain of living with a double identity and talked about the need to go home every so often, to "touch base with my own world, to check out my perspectives," and, most of all, "to be able to talk to people without having to explain everything." As she said, "the sheer energy required for living in two cultures" wore her down, and she needed to take time out to relax and be herself. "Home is a great place to run away from as long as you can go back once in a while."

The ideal, of course, is to be an expatriate spouse who somehow manages to blend the two cultures, the one born into and the one married into, and to form a new, third culture which builds on the others. This takes an exceptionally strong sense of self to begin with and a positive attitude toward the partner's culture, as well as a willingness to continually grow. It also takes a partner who is equally self-confident and appreciative of the "otherness" of the foreign spouse.

Mary and Bill who met while graduate students at the University of California, Berkeley, truly liked as well as loved each other, and, standing together to withstand the prejudices of the outside world towards their intercultural-interracial marriage, they managed to allow each other to grow within their marriage. Bill was grateful that Mary was an independent, resilient woman and stuck with her while she struggled with the dilemma of how to enculturate without losing herself.

This dilemma is beautifully stated by another expatriate spouse, the writer Ruth Prawer Jhabvala. German-born and

English-educated, Jhabvala married an Indian architect and followed him to New Delhi where she lived for over twenty years:

> "To live in India and be at peace, one must to a very considerable extent become Indian and adopt Indian attitudes, habits, beliefs, assume if possible an Indian personality. But how is this possible? And even if it were possible—without cheating oneself—would it be desirable? Should one want to try to become something other than what one is? I don't always say no to this question. Sometimes it seems to me how pleasant it would be to say yes and give in and wear a sari and be meek and accepting and see God in a cow. Other times it seems worthwhile to be defiant and European and—all right, be crushed by one's environment, but all the same have made some attempt to remain standing."[36]

[36] Ruth Prawer Jhabvala, *Out of India*, p 21.

MAKING MIRACLES ISN'T EASY

PART 3

MANAGING THE DIFFERENCES

In the preceding sections we have looked at how difficulties emerge for intercultural couples because of the differences in their backgrounds. In the third part of this book we change our focus, moving from listing the problems to focusing on ways of dealing with the differences, of predictors of a successful relationship, and some things to think about before marriage.

At this point, we need to add a note of caution. In this section we are going to concentrate on ways of managing these differences, but we want to make it clear that we certainly don't claim to have all the answers. There is no blueprint for success, no one right way. Although some solutions work better than others, ideally speaking, the only right solution is the one that works for each couple. Our ideal solution is only ideal from our point of view, but may be neither possible nor desirable for others.

First we'll outline a few types of intercultural marital models: arrangements different couples have found as ways of handling their differences within the marital unit. We'll see how the most successful couples allow for each other's differentness without losing their own. We will see how those couples combine what is the best of both cultures into their marriages and achieve the near-perfect balance.

Then we will list the factors to which the couples themselves attribute their successes, and show some of the commonalities of the successful couples.

Finally, we will compile the advice the many couples interviewed for this book gave to those who might be considering intercultural marriage (or are at the beginning of their lives together), and we will look at particular things intercultural couples would be wise to consider before marrying, one of them being the special problems which arise when the marriage is over—through separation, death or divorce.

TYPES OF INTERCULTURAL MARRIAGES

 Couple

 She

 He

Couples have their own systems for working out the power balance in their relationships, for deciding who gives and who takes. Some are more successful than others. These systems generally fall into one, or a combination, of four types of marital models: submission, compromise, obliteration, or consensus.

Submission

The most frequent (and for many people the most successful) marital model is that in which one partner submits to the culture of the other partner, abandoning or denying his or her own in doing so.

To many intercultural couples, submission of one partner to the culture of the other is the best or only way for these marriages to survive because it nullifies cultural conflict. Most of the time it is the woman who defers to the man's culture because, traditionally, even in the most progressive of societies, the responsibility for the relationship is laid at the feet of the woman—it is she who is expected to adapt to the man and his culture. In some cases, especially when the woman is from a male-dominant culture herself, submitting to the man and his culture is the most natural thing in the world for her to do, part of her duty as a wife.

Often one partner submits because one culture is so dominant or exclusive that it allows for no alternative. This is especially true in countries in which religion regulates most behaviors. Submission may be merely superficial, however—for public appearance—while in their private life the couple maintains a more balanced relationship. In other situations the personality of one partner may be so dominant that it forces submission allowing for little freedom on the part of the other. Often one partner is drawn to and identifies with the other culture (or wants to escape from his or her own) so strongly that the choice to identify with it totally is freely made.

However, despite the many advocates of the submission-submersion model, it has definite disadvantages. A person is never totally successful at denying or losing his/her ethnic identity. Sometimes it seems to work well at first, especially if it is the woman who submits, if she is from a male-dominant culture, if she is younger or more dependent by nature than the man, if she is a newcomer to the culture and insecure in its ways, or if she submits willingly to the other culture.

Rarely does this model work in the long run, however. People cannot stop seeing the world or measuring it according to their own yardstick. They cannot erase the core of their being. Most likely a certain resentment will slowly eat away at them until sooner or later (often years later) it has to come to the surface and be dealt with.

Compromise

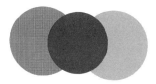

Another way couples may handle their cultural differences is through compromise. In this kind of arrangement, each partner gives up certain (often important) aspects of his or her culturally-bound habits and beliefs to make room for the habits and beliefs of the other.

Theoretically, this is a good solution as it indicates equality in the relationship—an important ingredient. It shows a sense of fairness, flexibility, and openness, all of which are essential to the success of intercultural relationships. Compromise means making trade-offs: "We'll bring the girls up Christian and the boys Muslim," for example, or "We'll send money to the Chinese relatives but take our vacations visiting the European ones." There is an adjustment made on the part of both. By its very definition *compromise* means "to adjust and settle differences by mutual agreement, with concessions on both sides."[37]

However, compromise can also mean "to endanger the interests of; to surrender or give up one's interests, principles, etc."[38] And here is the less desirable aspect of compromise. In the intercultural marriage what it often really means is that there has been an adjustment (or sacrifice) made for the sake of coexistence, which satisfies neither partner. Both have won a little, but both have lost a little too, and sometimes the things which have been compromised are things which really mattered to one or the other of the partners. The Englishman who has given up his plum pudding at Christmas may really begrudge

[37] Webster's *Unabridged Dictionary, op. cit.*.
[38] *Ibid.*

giving it up. If this is the case, then no one is really happy. The issues are never really resolved but resurface again and again to be renegotiated or argued over.

Many couples, however, consider this compromise type of marital contract better than no give-and-take at all. Both can claim to have done their part towards making the marriage work. If they keep at it long enough (changing the details back and forth), they may eventually reach a compromise satisfying to both (which we are calling consensus).

Obliteration

Obliteration refers to the kind of marital model in which couples try to manage their differences by erasing them, by denying their individual cultures altogether. These third-culture couples form a new cultural identity which has no memories, no traditions, no cultural causes for conflict. They often give up their languages, life-styles, customs and even their beliefs and values. In a sense they run away from potential conflicts.

For some couples this is indeed the only solution because their cultures are so drastically different that there is no alternative. There are, for example, the Romeo and Juliet couples, who come from warring or enemy nations and escape to a neutral third country which they adopt as their own, assuming as much of its identity as possible. Sometimes the couples meet in the third country, remain there, and bring their children up as natives of that country, far away from the critical eyes of their own families and friends, and the rules and customs of their own lands.

This sometimes works, but it is not an ideal solution

because it implies a loss for both partners—perhaps willingly accepted in order to be together, but a loss nonetheless.

In the obliteration model both partners have sacrificed and/or lost their ethnic heritages; they have renounced an important part of themselves and denied their children the warmth and richness of their cultures. They are "culture-poor," often without any kind of support system or any sense of truly belonging. As McGoldrick, Pearce, and Giordano point out,[39] a sense of belonging and of historical continuity is a basic psychological need. We may ignore it or cut it off by changing our names and rejecting our families and social background, but we do so to the detriment of our well-being.

Consensus

If we were to choose an ideal intercultural marriage model, we would be inclined to say that it is one based on consensus, i.e. agreement. Consensus is related to compromise in that it implies a give-and-take on the part of both partners; but it is different in that it is not a trade-off but an agreement, and no scores are kept.

In a consensus model neither partner sacrifices things which are essential to his or her well-being—as often happens in the other situations. Both are whole people and whole partners, with a solid sense of self, of their own differentness, and their individual needs, values and expectations for which they are willing to fight. Both are strong and secure enough in themselves to allow their partners to be different without considering it a betrayal or a threat. They are able to give to one

[39] *Ethnicity and Family Therapy,* p 5.

another—whenever and wherever the need is greatest—spontaneously, willingly, and without keeping count.

The consensus relationship is a win-win relationship. As Mahatma Gandhi put it, winning is never simply a matter of conquest; winning "requires a transformation of relationships."[40]

An example of this kind of marriage was provided by Jehan Sadat, wife of the Egyptian leader, Anwar Sadat, when she described the intercultural marriage (her mother was British) of her parents.

> My mother really sacrificed herself.... She left her country, her family, her friends. She left everything because she loved my father... and she came to my country with different traditions, different customs. And of course she was shocked when she arrived, and she was shocked even later on, until the last moment of her life. She ate the British kind of food. She never touched our kind of cooking. And my father, who was a typical Egyptian man, also never changed his way of life. But what combined them really was love. Love made such a miracle for both of them; it made their lives and their marriage.

> My father was Muslim. She was not. She had a great respect for my father.... My father never told her to change her religion, to become Muslim. She never thought of converting, but she was very concerned about us children as Muslims. She used to watch to be sure we fasted during Ramadan. She used to share the fast with us when we were grown up.

> She loved her husband, she loved her Egyptian family, but at the same time she adored her country.[41]

As Jehan Sadat said, "Love makes miracles,"—but so do people. Making miracles, however, isn't easy. It takes work and causes stress. People who want their intercultural marriages to work must be prepared for this. The couple who will come

---

[40] Taken from Mark Juergensmeyer, *Fighting with Gandhi*, p 59.
[41] Quoted from an article by Prince Michael in *Parade Magazine*, July 14, 1985.

closest to an ideal intercultural marriage is the one ready to face the issues and fight them out, over and over again if necessary, even if it causes stress. To risk facing the pitfalls may be dangerous but it is the only way to gain the opportunity to fulfill the promises and to grow together in an ever-expanding, enriching relationship.[42]

FACTORS FOR SUCCESS

Some intercultural marriages are successes. Others falter along the way. Many endure. Some fail. The success or failure of the marriage is in the end a personal matter, depending on the two people involved. But there are certain characteristics which, to a greater or lesser degree, we found common among couples whose marriages worked.

Any list is somewhat arbitrary and this is no exception. Usually couples placed most emphasis on one or two things; the others either seemed less important or were difficult to attain. Few of the couples could claim to have all the factors going for them, but the more successful couples had enough of them to keep their marriages on a solid footing while they worked on the others. There are ten:

1. Good motives for the marriage

2. Common goals

3. Sensitivity to each other's needs

4. A liking for the other's culture

5. Flexibility

6. Solid, positive self-image

---

[42] Ideas for this section are based on the concept of "satyagraha" (truth force) as expressed in *Fighting with Gandhi.*

7.   Spirit of adventure

8.   Ability to communicate

9.   Commitment to the relationship

10.   Sense of humor

Good Motives for the Marriage

Love is usually at the center of the reason two people choose to marry one another, but love in the *true* sense—not the passionate or romantic sense. Insofar as love means that which makes two people want to live together "for the mutual goal of forming a family to stabilize and improve the quality of their life,"[43] it is a valid motive for marriage. Insofar as it means both spouses wanting to help their partners fulfill themselves in their own way, love is the best motive for the intercultural marriage.

In such a marriage the emotional energy behind the decision is all important. If one or both of the spouses enters into the marriage for other reasons, the marriage will most likely be dysfunctional. This is not to say the marriage won't work if other motives were behind the decision, but interpersonal problems are more likely to be encountered.

Adela and Mohammed, for example, basically had a dysfunctional marriage. He had never accepted her for what she was. He wanted her to become a Muslim according to *his* interpretation of the dictates of his faith. He was convinced that it was for her own good, that it was his duty as her husband and religious mentor to insist on his way. He believed he was merely helping her find her best self; but, in actuality, he was denying her the right, the duty and the opportunity to fulfill herself in her own way.

Adela, on the other hand, let herself be coerced. She

---

[43] *Adjustments in Intercultural Marriage,* op. cit., p 101.

thought she had found the answers to life in Mohammed. She converted to his faith in an honest desire to believe and to find herself, but also to please him, though it was this latter motive that was the strongest.

As time passed, she turned to deceit and trickery to avoid confrontation and subtly tried to dissuade Mohammed from too rigid an adherence to his beliefs. He turned more and more to coercion, and both of them lived with a sense of failure in their marriage.

Few people are selfless enough to want only what is best for the other (especially if that conflicts with their own wants and needs), and married life is generally a continuous search to find the right balance between what both want for themselves and what both can put up with in the other. But if their fundamental motive for marriage is strong and valid, they find the right balance. The longer and more honestly they search together for this balance, the closer they will become.

Common Goals

Whenever both husband and wife want essentially the same things out of life, they will probably find a way to work together towards those ends, despite the difference in their methods of achieving them.

This is a delicate area because it is so closely tied to basic value orientations. While it is obviously easier if the two partners share the same basic values, it is not impossible for the marriage to succeed if their orientations are not the same; but it requires a stronger bond of love between them. Even where the values differ, two people can have the same personal and relational goals.

Kimberly and Louis could not have been more different in their cultural backgrounds and orientations. But both felt strongly about one matter: both wanted and needed a solid family unit. Louis had lost his family in Cambodia, Kimberly lost hers through divorce; and they were determined that their family would endure. This determination was their driving force, and they hacked away at all the differences and difficulties which threatened them, never losing sight of their primary goal. They managed to overcome difficulties caused by their cultural differences because of this common goal, and they grew stronger in the process.

Less noble, but no less of a driving force, was the common goal which bound Fiamma, the Italian jet-set communist, and her English husband, Andrew. Both were dedicated to enabling Andrew to earn lots of money for them to spend in order to establish and maintain themselves in an international circle. They didn't want to be confined by values, rules or obligations. Whatever got in the way of this goal, they eliminated, which included many old friends, being together (Andrew traveled eight months out of the year), and associating with their elderly (but socially unacceptable) parents.

While it cannot be said that they were particularly happy people or had an ideal marriage, their dedication to this common goal tied them together.

Sensitivity to Each Other's Needs

Although this is the third factor on our list, it could be the first because without it a marriage is lifeless. Being sensitive means being able to feel or perceive and respond to outside stimuli, in this case the other's needs, which may be emotional or physical, personal or cultural. For the intercultural couple, it also means being cross-culturally aware and empathetic. It means learning to understand the other's values, beliefs, and needs, comprehending how the other interprets life and its meaning, and being able to learn how to feel the way the other feels.

If the two partners do not share each other's beliefs and values, they must learn to understand and respect them and accept them as different but equally valid *for the other person.* Only in that way will they be able to help one another achieve their goals. This means that they have to be givers as well as takers in the relationship and that what they must be willing to give their partner is the leeway to be different.

Harry had to learn not only to understand that Milee was different from his hearty, jovial friends and that she was offended by what she saw as their rudeness and cruel, joking manners, but he also had to actually feel her embarrassment when someone gave her a big hug and to suffer for her, whether he agreed with her reactions or not. In time he learned to understand that she needed to associate with people from her own country who saw life as she saw it and to support those friendships. Milee, on the other hand, learned to stop seeing Harry as insensitive just because he could not read her thoughts and interpret her nonverbal messages. She learned to know when he needed to hear her speak of her love for him and to explain verbally what she wanted of him as a partner and what she expected from their relationship.

Yvette learned to understand Ali's displeasure when she attracted the attention of men on the street because she was dressed in jeans or other inappropriate Western-style dress and to respect his desire that she conform, at least outwardly, to the customs of his country. She learned to cater to him with the domestic pampering which he required as an expression of her love. Ali empathized with Yvette's discontent over not being able to make a real career for herself in his country, though he himself did not consider careers to be important ingredients for women's happiness. But he came to accept that Yvette was different from Kuwaiti women, and that her needs were different from theirs; she needed to succeed on her own, for herself, not only as wife and mother. He learned to understand and feel her frustration and to help her further her personal goals when he could.

On the other hand, Olu was never able to submit to Rashida's demands to live her life to its fullest, according to her own ideals. Finally, he repudiated her as an unfit wife and divorced her.

A Liking for the Other's Culture

It is rarely possible to allow for or accept the other partner's needs if there is a basic dislike of the other's culture.

We are products of our cultures, and if our partners disparage our race, nationality, religion, or way of life, an underlying contempt will always separate them from us.

This is not to say that the partners have to like *everything* about the other's culture, but they should like enough of it to be able them to overlook or accept the parts they do not.

Miguel liked very little about Carol's American culture. He didn't like its politics; he criticized its work ethic; he found Americans to be rude, classless, money-hungry, superficial people. His dislike prevented him from looking beneath the surface to discover the good qualities of the country or the similarities between it and his own Chile. His most devastating putdown to his wife was, "You're acting like a typical American." Carol knew her country was less than perfect, but it was hers to criticize, hers to hate at times, *not his!* She took his criticisms personally, as criticisms of herself—as of course they were in part. His antipathy towards everything American and her resentment of that criticism created a problem for them in the years they were together.

On the other hand, Lynn and Hans both liked and were attracted to the cultures of the other. Both quietly believed in the superiority of most aspects of their own culture, but were open to integrating many aspects of the other into their lifestyles.

Lynn loved the physical beauty of her adopted country, the simplicity of life in the mountain village, the kindness of Hans' friends, who had gone out of their way to help her adjust to marriage in this new land, and she loved the solid practicality of her handsome husband. Hans was fascinated by everything American. He became a fan of peanut butter and brownies; he loved his wife's American optimism and her confidence that anything she set her mind to was possible, her outgoing friendliness, and her ability to giggle at her own foolish mistakes.

Many of the qualities they attributed to each other were not necessarily cultural characteristics, but their positive attitudes towards each other's cultures made them see these as such.

Flexibility

Being flexible means being able to adjust, being open to trying something new and different, being willing to consider that there might be a valid alternative to the way one is used to doing or seeing things.

In intercultural marriages flexibility is an essential character trait of the successful spouse. Inflexible people are takers: they force the other to do the giving, the changing, the adjusting in marriage. Generally they are insensitive to the other partner's needs and selfish in pursuing their personal goals, insisting that these become their partner's goals as well. They take themselves too seriously and usually are not much fun.

Being flexible means being like a reed swaying in the wind, bending this way or that, according to the need: pliable and strong, able to withstand the strain of sudden changes, unexpected events, or tough times without being uprooted or broken. A successful intercultural marriage is one which is made up of two flexible people who both take the time and make the effort to learn and to understand as much as possible about the other's culture and are open to trying out different aspects of it in their own life-styles. Flexible couples will be able to tolerate the confusion their two different ways of living bring into their daily routine. They are able to work through sensitive problems that can cause hurt feelings until they negotiate an agreement which hurts no one.

When Rosemary and Ravi lived in Canada, Rosemary enjoyed making superficial adjustments to his culture. She wore saris and cooked Indian food on occasion. She studied the language and the art. She was fascinated by the mysticism and the culture of the Indian people. But Ravi made all the other changes—the really big ones. He adapted to Western ways of socializing, to the Western work ethic and time orientation, and to the Westerner's haphazard neglect of what he considered basic courtesies. He preferred his own ways; he was convinced of their superiority, but he adapted.

When they went to live in India, he expected Rosemary to do the same thing—to adjust to his ways as he had adapted to hers. Now it was her turn to do more than put on the costume and assume the pose. But as time passed, both realized that Rosemary was having trouble adjusting—she felt she was being asked to give up too much. She missed the privacy of her own home; she resented the influence of his ever present family on their domestic lives; she strained under the psychological hardships of living in a land of famine and poverty.

Both finally recognized their limitations and realized that they were going to have to find another solution, one not based on "his turn, her turn." They were wise enough to know that her inability to adjust to his land had nothing to do with her love for him. Ravi knew that he was going to have to give up a little more of his own culture because he was more able to do so than she was, and he was flexible enough to do it without keeping score.

Fortunately, Ravi was able to arrange a posting outside India, this time to West Germany. Once they moved, Rosemary returned to loving all things Indian, to wearing her saris and to making Indian friends in Bonn (or wherever else they were transferred). She even taught a course in Indian art to the English-speaking women's club. India was wonderful—so long as she didn't have to live there.

Solid, Positive Self-Image

As we have seen with Rosemary and Ravi, being flexible takes a person with a strong sense of self-worth. People without this sense feel threatened by difference, by nonconformity, and are unable to risk trying something which is not familiar. They want the other partner to be the one who adjusts to *their* familiar and comfortable ways so their security isn't threatened.

Most of the people who marry interculturally feel they are, in one way or another, unlike their compatriots who marry people from similar backgrounds. Most of those we interviewed for this book described themselves as different or special in one way or another. Almost all of the spouses, and especially the ones who were in what they themselves considered successful marriages, felt they were not only different, but also "above the norm." When they are in fact above the norm, in the sense of having a very strong self-image, they do seem to have a higher rate of success.

Tove was an only child, bicultural herself, the daughter of a successful businessman. Massimo was the eldest in his family, part of the respected diplomatic world. Rosemary was the baby, the child who came along many years after the others and was the center of everyone's attention. Ravi was the eldest child and the recipient of a Fulbright Fellowship. Kimberly was the daughter of a rabbi. Bill was an accomplished musician. Mary was the daughter of a tribal chief. Louis was an accomplished graphic artist. Ikumi had a law degree, and Zehyra was physically a very beautiful woman. Harry was a successful journalist, and Hiroshi was a distinguished university professor.

All were solid, optimistic people who felt good about themselves and the way they were handling their lives. They liked their own uniqueness, and they liked the specialness their marriages gave them. They knew their limitations and had a sense of what was essential and what they could let go of. They knew who they were and basically liked themselves.

This is not to say that they started out this way, but that they had enough seeds of confidence in themselves before their marriages to be able to search with their partners for solutions to the particular problems encountered. Accepting themselves enabled them to accept the other and to grow together despite their differences.

Spirit of Adventure

Part of what makes these spouses the special people they are is another shared characteristic: the spirit of adventure and curiosity about the world.

The successful spouses almost all said they were looking for more out of life than the familiar routine which marrying their own kind would have given them. They didn't intentionally set out to find someone of another culture to marry, but they were open to the idea and ready for the adventure of it when the possibility came their way.

Often they met the foreigners they did because of this very spirit, because they put themselves in a position to meet all kinds of people. Many met while traveling, studying, or working abroad. Others in their own homelands sought out the company of a wider range of people and so met their future foreign partners. Some met by accident but were curious or adventuresome enough to be open to the relationship.

However, the spirit which impelled them into their intercultural marriages was not a youthful passing phase. It was something which remained with them during their married lives and helped them confront the unexpected events of their cross-cultural existence, the ambiguities and the sense of unreality which can accompany this kind of married life. A sense of adventure is enriching when the motives are positive.

It is a trait shared by all the couples interviewed, but some, like Helga with her Libyan activist husband; Esmeralda, with her Brazilian soccer player; and Jeanpierre, with Anne, the family's Ethiopian maid, were adventurer types who were also escapists or unstable people and had few of the other qualities necessary for success. And their marriages lasted only as long as their rebelliousness.

For many others this innate sense of adventure served them well through some of the more challenging moments of their marriages. Ikumi recalled that as a child she always "looked for dares, loved taking risks, was afraid of nothing." As a bride-to-be, she was saddened but not afraid of the threats made by her parents to keep her from marrying Cecil. This same spirit helped her cross over the double bridge her marriage presented: leaving her family, both physically and spiritually, and stepping into the new and totally different Western culture. It permitted her to follow Cecil willingly to postings around the world, even to some that were not very attractive. It helped her recover after her near breakdown when she had to leave Bangladesh and return to her parents' home and beg them to take her in until she was able to regain her health. It gave her courage to try again.

Victor had to overcome much of his Swiss-German fastidiousness whenever his Tunisian in-laws visited or when he spent time in their country. It wasn't just the food, but also many of the diverse customs which he found difficult to digest. (He became quite fond of Zehyra's Tunisian stews—but never quite managed the goat's eye.) Zehyra felt that her marriage was a natural outcome of her personality. She had festered under Tunisia's suppression of females and felt she had improved her way of life by marrying into the Swiss culture. But, nevertheless, it took time to learn to cope with the new freedoms she found with Victor. Without her spirit of adventure, she would not have been as ready to turn her back on everyone and everything she knew to get the kind of life she wanted.

None of these adventuresome spouses are boring people; in fact they all abhor dullness. When they talk about their marriages, they may describe them in many ways: good or bad, difficult or fun, stressful, complicated, unpredictable, etc. But they will be quick to add that, at least they are never, ever boring.

Ability to Communicate

We have seen in the chapter on language and communication how many obstacles there are to the effective sharing of messages between partners from different cultures, often beginning with the languages they speak and their different styles of behaving and relating. Yet most of the couples cited the ability to communicate as being one of the most essential ingredients of success in marriage, though admitting that it took a lot of work, patience and care.

It doesn't seem to matter whether the dominant style of managing communication is verbal or nonverbal or whether or not it is peaceful. The important thing is managing somehow to understand and be understood by each other. Almost all the successful couples made an attempt to learn one another's language, but, more important, they learned one another's style of communicating and used it (if not always comfortably) to get their messages across. Both partners were prepared to do their share of reaching out. They were prepared for the occasional perceptual blackouts which occur and were ready to negotiate and try again. Both were committed to succeeding. Only one assumption was allowed: that clarification would probably be needed somewhere along the line.

Something few of them actually identified, but which was universally present in the better communicators, was clarity of thought: they themselves knew what they were trying to say and so were able to keep at it until they were sure that they had communicated the right message. Those who were less clear in their own minds (especially regarding what they expected from one another and what they wanted from the relationship) had a harder time communicating.

Deirdre and Mario, for example, were searching for themselves, unsure of what they really wanted from one another and from their lives, and so were unable to send clear messages to each other.

Cassie and Jaime, on the other hand, despite their very different cultures, personalities and interests, learned in time to fight for what they wanted and needed from life and from one another. They described themselves as fighting "like cats and dogs" and did not see themselves as effective communicators. But the more they thought about it, the more they realized that although they rarely agreed, at least they understood one another and admitted that this was progress. They had come a long way from their early days.

Commitment to the Relationship

One thing most couples felt helped them over the bumps was their commitment to the success of the marriage as well as to each other. Most felt that intercultural spouses try harder than those in monocultural marriages; that they not only have a higher degree of tolerance, but that they expect from the very beginning that there will be difficulties because of the differences between them. They believe they are more prepared to make allowances for imperfections or failures than are monocultural couples.

Sometimes their commitment to the marriage has something to do with pride. Many of these marriages have taken place against the advice of family and friends. The spouses have left the fold and are occasionally disowned or repudiated by their families, or suspected of being socially deviant. They need to prove to everyone (sometimes themselves included) that what they did was right. It's hard to admit that they might have made a mistake—that everyone else might have been right—and face the spoken or implied "I told you sos" back home. So, when faced with the prospect of marital breakdown, they have another try at working it out.

There might also be a reluctance to give up the new identity, the uniqueness they acquired through the marriage. It's hard to go back to being just like everyone else, especially for those who need to be different, who perhaps were escaping from something they didn't like in their own culture by marrying out of it. Often the same motives which led them into the marriage in the first place keep them working at it when the relationship goes sour.

However, a marriage commitment is often interpreted differently by people from different cultures. Some feel that it means an all-inclusive devotion to and responsibility for the well-being of each other, while others consider the first responsibility to be to themselves and leave the relationship to somehow take care of itself.

Mohammed thought he was being a good husband by controlling his wife's activities and monitoring her spiritual and physical well-being, and he expected and required the same kind of devotion from her. Adela's Cuban background had prepared her for dedicating herself to her family, but she had trouble with the all-inclusiveness of the commitment he required. But as in everything else, she submitted to his wish, though reluctantly.

Massimo and Tove were both committed to the bond which united them while they independently pursued their own kind of fulfillment. Massimo, when he wasn't working, was squirreled away with his manuscripts, with his nose in his research, or hunched over his typewriter. He had his circle of friends who Tove liked but found too "egg-headed" for her personal taste. She managed to find clubs and charity work to be involved in wherever they were posted and kept busy with bridge tournaments and "juicy gossip." But both enjoyed the variety their differing interests brought into their married life; neither felt threatened by the fact that the other looked outside as well as inside the marriage for fulfillment. Their marriage was based not only on enjoyment of what made the other different and on trust that that "otherness" would not divide them, but also on a similar interpretation of the kind of commitment they wanted and expected from one another.

Despite the pulls of their various cultures and perhaps because of the obstacles they had to overcome to be together, most of the couples were more committed to their immediate than to their extended families. This was more natural for some than others, but even those whose cultures dictated total filial devotion and responsibility moved somewhat away from a strict adherence to this rule. They did not necessarily cut themselves off from their extended families, but tended to place more emphasis on the obligations to their own spouse and children.

As Malaysian Rani explained it, "When I married Sune, I left my family. This is one of the reasons they objected and cried at the time of my marriage, because they knew they were losing me more than if I had married someone of my own kind. But it was my choice and is my obligation. Sune and my children come first."

Sense of Humor

The last factor for success, a sense of humor, is the one most of the couples agree is important when all else fails, and yet it is the most culturally-bound factor. What makes one person laugh leaves the other indifferent, confused, or perhaps offended. Still, the couples agreed that those who found their own "home humor" and built up their own repertoires of funny incidents had a better chance of getting over the hard times.

Knowing how to laugh—especially at themselves and at their mistakes as bumbling culture-crossers—takes away some of the tension and gives them time out to pause and think things through. A humorous interlude helps them remember what binds them together in the midst of their differences. It helps them remember that they entered these marriages, not only for all the serious things that attracted them, but also because the marriage promised to be fun.

BEFORE TAKING THAT BIG STEP

Hope for the best and prepare for the worst.

—Anonymous

In the preceding chapters we have learned some of the things which make intercultural marriage special. Although this book is certainly not meant to discourage people from entering intercultural marriages, it is meant to suggest that they may not be for everyone and that people should take every opportunity beforehand to find out what they are getting into.

Being in love is not enough to make these marriages work. There are many questions future spouses should ask themselves regarding their capacity to cope. There are questions they should also ask the person they love in order to evaluate them as future partners before deciding whether or not intercultural marriage (or intercultural marriage with *that* person) is for them.

Love is blind, it is said. International love is further handicapped because the cultural differences between the two lovers can distort perception. These people have to make a more concerted and conscious effort to know one another by finding out as much as possible about the other's culture and to know themselves by redefining what is and is not necessary for their happiness.

Generally when two people from different cultures meet and begin to date, they are so busy figuring out the logistics of wooing and winning one another that they may find themselves at the threshold of their wedding without having explored the issues which will turn up in their marriage, the issues discussed in part two.

We would like to offer suggestions for prospective spouses before they leap into marriage with someone from another culture. We plan to do this by dividing these suggestions into two categories: (1) things to do that will help the couple learn about one another and about each other's culture, and (2) things to *consider* carefully before deciding to marry.

Things To Do

Experiment with a Trial Run: Live Together. Some couples feel that if they live together in a sort of trial run, they will find out how well both their personalities and their cultures mesh. Certainly this is one possibility. But, for any number of reasons, it is neither desirable nor possible for everyone. Living together is not an infallible way to test a relationship because that "little piece of paper," which pronounces a man and woman husband and wife, is not merely symbolic; it actually changes the relationship. The new roles and the sense of the permanence of the situation can make previously tolerated traits unbearable; it can make people change their demands and expectations.

Also, before the marriage frequently one or both of the partners is living in a foreign country; upon returning home, his/

her behavior may radically change—often to the surprise and shock of the other.

Make a Home Visit. Although this may be difficult or impossible in many situations for financial as well as other reasons, the best prenuptial preparation for bicultural couples is for each to have an opportunity to live with, or visit for an extended period of time, the future spouse's family before the wedding. Not only will they have an opportunity to see in action the family which molded the partner, but they will also have the experience of being immersed in the other's culture. This is especially useful for the man or woman who has been in his or her own homeland for the courtship period or who will possibly be moving to the other country when married. Both will have a chance to see how well the future partner fits in with the other's family and culture.

By living with the family (assuming language is not a barrier) the visitor can see what the family is like without company manners and what customs the family and culture adhere to. This is the time to learn about how decisions are made (and who makes them), how family members relate to one another, how male/female roles are defined, how and to what extent the extended family is included in their lives, how generations relate to each other, how love and affection are expressed, how arguments are dealt with, how parents punish the children, how conflicts are resolved, and how courtesy and respect are displayed. Living with the family will reveal more about how they interact with one another than a thousand discussions.

The visit will provide a social picture of the family: who their friends are and how they define friendship; how they regard work and handle finances, and what they consider fun; how they entertain; what kind of library they have; what sort of vacations they like; what kind of house or apartment they live in with what furnishings; and how much or little importance they give (and how they define) such things as cleanliness and hygiene. Finally, an observant guest can gain at least a partial understanding of the family's attitudes regarding sex, marriage and religion.

Living with the family will not only reveal to the prospective spouse what it is that helped form the future partner's character, but will also give a good indication of what patterns of behavior are likely to emerge once they are married and establishing a home and family of their own.

The spouses who will become expatriates upon marrying benefit the most from living with the other's family beforehand because it provides an opportunity to see how well they can cope with living in the other culture and with being far away from home, family, friends and familiar support systems; they will also certainly get a feeling for how well they can expect to get along with their future in-laws.

Socialize with the Partner's Friends. Unfortunately, since the home visit to the future spouse's family is an impossible luxury for many, the next best thing is for both people to meet and spend as much time as possible with one another's friends. Couples in love, especially at first, tend to spend all their time alone together. In marriage this isolation usually ends, so it makes sense to get to know one another's friends *before* the wedding, when they can serve as both companions and culture interpreters.

Friends can help these people from different backgrounds learn about one another almost as much as families can. Sometimes people act one way in new surroundings (because they believe it is what is expected of them) and another way when they are with their own people. An alert culture-observer will notice these differences and what they mean. He/she will see what makes the friends laugh when they are together and what they take seriously and will note how that differs from his or her own group. The future spouse will also note whether the fiancé(e) expects to be treated differently when with his/her friends; if so, that is the time to ask why. An alert observer can also learn about the friends' attitudes toward religion, morality, dating, marriage, divorce, families, birth control, equality of the sexes, etc.

Friends can also show how social relationships are carried on in the other culture. Do men have only men friends and women, women? Do the sexes mix comfortably with one another in open or nonflirtatious ways? If they do flirt, what are the rules? How well is the foreigner accepted among the friends and what are their attitudes towards the foreigner's culture? What do they do together to have fun? What kind of music do they like? What do they talk about? What social graces are important? How do men show courtesy to women, women to men, and both to elders? One can also learn a great deal about communication in the partner's culture: do people embrace one another, do they stand close or far apart when conversing, how do they use gestures, touching, eye contact, and tone of voice to communicate?

Friends are an invaluable resource for intercultural couples. A fair rule of thumb: if you fit in with the friends, you will fit in with the culture, and you will have a better than average chance of adapting to one another.

Learn the Language. Knowing the partner's language is important for many reasons. First, communicating with friends and family of the fiancé(e) often requires speaking their language. Even if they speak both languages, a knowledge of their language helps you to know them in depth, to see them at ease in their own language, and to be able to participate in their world more fully.

Second, knowing the language opens up other means of learning about the partner's culture. It permits access to books, magazines, films, and TV programs. It means access to the humor and richness of the spoken language, the subtleties of the nonverbal language, and the communication style of the culture in general and the spouse in particular.

Most important, it helps the future spouses know one another more completely. Although many couples spend a lifetime together successfully, without knowing the other's language (especially if one partner is fluent in both), not making an effort to learn the language is eliminating one opportunity to know the other more fully, cutting off one source of understanding. Studying one another's language helps the spouses to interpret one another better. Not knowing it is like having a beautiful book, which one loves and cherishes, but can't read...and that's a pity.

Read and Go to Movies. Those couples with a working knowledge of one another's language can make use of the newspapers, magazines, books and films of the other's country to learn more about his or her culture.

Future partners can learn a great deal about the internal issues of the country, about its political as well as its social and economic situation from newspapers. They can learn what the problems are, the kinds of crimes committed, and the kinds of controls enacted. A lot can be learned by just finding out what is considered news. Newspapers also tell about the life-style and interests of the people of the country. An observant reader can find out what the country's attitude is toward his/her own country, how he/she will be looked upon by the natives, the extent of freedom of speech. Are there, for instance, articles critical of the government or military; is there coverage of politically unfavorable events?

Magazines can serve much the same purpose, but somewhat more in depth. They can show the deeper as well as the lighter side of the culture, the fads, the stars, the sports that are popular, how people dress, decorate their homes, and spend their leisure time.

Books serve as indicators of the more lasting character of a people: customs, attitudes, prejudices, problems, morals, beliefs, and values. Books are also an indicator of whether writers and artists are allowed freedom of expression or are censored.

Seeing films about the country, or which were produced there, also helps the prospective spouse learn about the manners, communication styles, interests, and living condition of the people. In films it is possible to *see* what the houses look like, how people dress, what kind of transportation exists, etc. (at least what the producers want viewers to see).

Study the Religion. If the two people are of different faiths, they should make a point of either taking religious instruction or individually studying each other's faith—even if they do not plan to convert. This is especially important if one partner is very devout or if one of the partners is planning to move to the country of the other, where one religion is dominant. Many cultures are tied up with the dominant religion, and a study of the history and dictates of the religion is a window on many aspects of the culture, including its values, rules, taboos, ceremonies and holidays. Study of the religion also gives an indication as to whether or not the foreigner will be accepted, whether he/she must convert, or raise their children in that faith. For couples who are nonpracticing, a study of the religion in which each of them was raised will give valuable insights into each other's background and character.

Eat the Cuisine. Potential partners who want to know as much as possible about each other's culture will leave no stone unturned. Seeking out and going to the restaurants which specialize in the partner's cuisine is another way to know the people. The smells of the food, the taste, the way the food is eaten, table manners, the interaction between natives and waiters all help in the learning process. If the couple is planning to move to one partner's country, the other partner would do well to make sure the food is at least tolerable, if not tasty. Other suggestions include checking out the kitchen (if possible) and the bathroom, and taking note of the decorations on the walls, the music playing, the way the table is set, etc. Small details may give hints about the customs, likes and dislikes of the people.

Search Out Resources. The partner who may be moving to the other's country upon marrying should seek to know as much as possible about the spouse's country by using available resources. History and guide books are helpful. A general encyclopedia article will give information about climate, economy, population, politics, areas of general interest, etc. Various organizations publish materials which also give general information about the people and the country, its laws and politics, its customs and climate (see bibliography for a selection of useful readings).

The prospective spouse's own government probably has an office which deals with the country he or she will be marrying into. The U.S. State Department, for example, has a "country desk" for each nation. The Office of Citizens Consular Services can also provide much of the information regarding the conditions, laws and customs of the land or can at least tell a future spouse where to go for that information.

The prospective spouse should also seek out people of his/her own county who have lived in the partner's country, people who will be able to pinpoint the differences and the difficulties, and give suggestions regarding how to handle the move. Women should find other women who can tell them about customs and possible restrictions and expectations regarding the woman's role in the country. Men should find other men who can tell them about the taboos, expectations, and duties which might be different from those of their own countries. If everyone says the same thing, it is probably true.

Another useful thing for these future wives and husbands to find out is whether or not there is a foreign community of their own nationals in the country, or if there are expatriate clubs or associations; and if there are, they should try to get in touch with them. These groups can provide up-to-date information and can make suggestions regarding what the new spouses should be prepared for, what they should bring with them, whether there is a place of worship for their own faith, etc. These groups can usually offer information about study, work and social activities as well. In other words, these organizations can provide a fairly accurate picture of the daily life: the specifics and details not obtainable in books or official documents.

Other intercultural couples, especially those with the same backgrounds, can be invaluable resources. But the new couple must be alert to distinguish between personal and cultural viewpoints and the possible prejudices which might bias any advice given; all information should be used with discretion. Many couples have joined cross-cultural support or discussion groups and benefited from listening to other couples who have gone before them, encountered problems, and dealt with them in their own style. The new couples found that the experience was invaluable, not only for specific suggestions they were able to pick up, but for the comfort it gave them to know that they were not alone, that others have been in similar quandaries and survived.

Try Games and Simulations. Once they have gotten a certain amount of information, the couple might try playacting living in the country of the other, as a husband/wife, according to the other's interpretation of the role. They should call upon all the details they have managed to acquire, as well as on any doubts, fears, and positive and negative cultural impressions they may have and use them in the playacting. They should try the role on for size and see how it fits. They should picture themselves in certain situations, imaginary or real, and see how they might cope. They can invent some specific incidents and figure out how to deal with them. This will open up other avenues of questions and perhaps doubts (as well as dispel certain misconceptions) about each other's cultures which they can then discuss together. In so doing, they will learn more about how each regards the other's culture and anticipates married life, as well as how each one tackles problems.

Some couples have found it amusing and informative to make a party game out of their explorations of each other's cultures. One couple had friends videotape them while they role-played possible situations which might be encountered in the other country: meeting relatives, shopping in the marketplace, serving dinner, wearing ceremonial dress, etc. They were able to see one another and, as an added benefit, note the different body language and other characteristics about themselves which the other constantly commented upon. This particular couple found that animated and invaluable discussions erupted when they played back the films and their friends took turns contributing comments and critiquing the performance. It was fun, funny and useful.

Consider Premarital Counseling. Sometimes premarital counseling is very helpful, especially if the couple manages to find someone who is versed in *cross-cultural* counseling. A good counselor can help the two people become culturally sensitive to each other and learn how to identify underlying problems and potential points of conflict. The couple can, with the help of a professional, get some perspective on these issues and learn how to work through them together. Learn to attack the issue, not each other, and to keep the two separate.

Not all cultures, however, are open to this kind of professional help-giving. If that is the case, the couple should seek out a respected elder, a religious leader or older friends who can help them deal with specific problems. The important thing here is to find someone familiar with both cultures who can interpret the partners correctly and not be hampered by his or her own cultural biases.

Things to Consider

Until this point we have concentrated on things intercultural couples can do to learn about each other and each other's culture. But there are a few other points the couple should investigate and consider before marrying.

Laws of the Land. Learning the laws of the land is an important part of preparing for marriage with someone from another country, especially if it is the couple's intention to reside there.

A good place to start is with each partner's own foreign ministry (in the U.S., the State Department) and with the embassy or consulate of the country to which they will be moving. Here answers can be obtained to basic enquiries regarding such things as visa requirements, residency restrictions, conditions for legalizing the marriage, etc. For example, it is not possible for future spouses to visit certain countries until they are actually married to each other.

If the couple is already living in the other country, the expatriate spouse should contact the consular section of his/her own embassy which specializes in citizen services; i.e. the section of the embassy which protects the welfare of its own citizens abroad. This office does such things as issue new passports and help stranded citizens return home. It often has the names of international lawyers who can help one learn about the laws which apply to people residing in that country or who marry one of its citizens. Its personnel have the answers to many questions which the future spouses frequently don't even know how to ask.

Citizenship. In some countries a bride or groom automatically becomes a citizen upon marrying. In others, the new spouse can apply for official residence immediately after the marriage and for citizenship status later. Some countries permit dual citizenship; others do not.

Children's citizenship. Will children be entitled to dual citizenship, and if so, how is it obtained? Will they be required to enter the armed forces of one or both countries? What restrictions are put upon their citizenship: special conditions which must be fulfilled, temporary duration (often countries require that children choose citizenship at age eighteen), and possible restrictions of movement in and out of the country?

Finances and taxation. What are the currency restrictions and taxes and how do they apply to foreign residents or dual citizens? For example, it is not legal to take more than a certain amount of money out of many countries. In other countries even income earned (or inherited) in another country is subject to taxation (sometimes resulting in double taxation).

Ownership of property. Can a foreigner buy, own and sell property? Can a woman? Can he/she dispose of it freely or is the cosignature of the spouse required? Would a will written in one country apply to properties held in another (most lawyers agree that it is best to have two wills—for property in each country)?

Other regulations. Must a foreign resident register with the police and get a local driver's license and identity card? Is free movement about the country permitted? Are there employment restrictions? Is a special work permit required? What are the laws regarding entitlement to a fair trial and legal representation in the case of suspected wrongdoing? How is insurance obtained: medical, life, home, etc.? What are the laws regarding divorce, custody of children, and inheritance?

Women's rights. Do women have freedom of movement? of dress? Can they be legally punished for infidelity or for refusing a husband his conjugal privileges? Can they own property in their own name and sign contracts for themselves, have their own checking accounts? Are they free agents with the same legal rights as their husbands, or are they subject to his authority? In some countries a woman cannot drive a car or travel outside its borders without the written consent of her husband.[44]

Do special limitations apply because they are of a different nationality (or religion), especially regarding custody of their children? In certain countries, a mother, if her faith is different from the dominant one, can lose her children to the father's family if something should happen to the father. What are the legal recourses in such a case? More than one mother has been known to flee a country and "kidnap" her children when she has been unable to take them out legally. The reverse happens too. Children have been "kidnapped" from the mother's country— even though a citizen of it—and taken to the father's where both are protected by the national laws.

Customs and Courtesies. Although not an essential consideration before marrying someone from a different culture, it is wise for those who will be residing in the other's country to learn its social customs and courtesies, if for no other reason than to better understand the behavior of the future partner.

There is no universal rule for appropriate social behavior, since customs are based on the values of a people. The rules vary greatly from culture to culture, and a newcomer must develop a keen sense of observation and sensitivity to hunt them out.

The best resource is the person's own partner, who has a vested interest in having the loved one judged well. But there are certain things which only women can or will tell other women and men other men. So it is wise to find a confidant in the other's country who will help by explaining how things are done or by pointing out errors (something which people of certain cultures will not do, at least not verbally.)

[44] Saudi Arabia, for example.

Advice columns (the "Dear Abbys") in the newspapers and magazines are other invaluable resources in these matters, as they are involved in teaching those who are unsure of the rules, themselves.

Divorce and Death. Although generally no one goes into these marriages thinking about getting out of them, some serious thought should be given to "what if." What if one were to lose one's spouse, either through death or divorce? Although these are two separate situations, with their own particular emotions and problems, both represent the loss of a spouse and share many similarities. For this reason we are going to consider them together.

The first thing for the expatriate spouse to find out is whether or not divorce exists in the country where the couple will be living. In Roman Catholic Argentina, Paraguay, Ireland, Malta and the Philippines, for example, divorce and remarriage are not permitted.

It is important to know the legal grounds for divorce and the rights of both partners afterwards. Under Muslim law, for example, a husband is permitted to divorce his wife without any legal procedure. Such divorce by *talak* merely requires him to state unequivocally three times his intention to repudiate the marriage. Although many countries now require that such a divorce be registered, the wife often has no recourse.[45]

Other important laws are those regarding custody, child support, alimony, property division and the continued residence of the divorced foreigner in the country. These laws differ widely from country to country and may be totally unlike what one is accustomed to.

For widows or widowers there are many rites and rituals which should be known and discussed before marriage. There are mourning and burial customs which may be difficult for someone brought up in a different culture, as well as laws specifically regarding widows after their husband's death. In

---

[45] According to the writings of the Ayatollah Khomeini, a Muslim man or woman may not marry a non-Muslim in continuing marriage; they may be joined only in temporary marriage.

some countries, for example, the widow must live with her husband's family, often becoming the wife of the brother-in-law—even if he already has one. In Zambia there is a "cleansing ritual" (officially frowned upon by the government but nonetheless still practiced) in which a widow must sleep with her brother-in-law in order to rid herself of her husband's ghost.

Special thought should be given to the problems of being a divorced or widowed foreigner in another country, both regarding the legal standing and the psychological/social connotations.

Although divorce or widowhood is easy for neither men nor women, it is perhaps most difficult for the expatriate wife who has left her home and friends and spent a lifetime in the husband's country. When alone, these women (especially in male-dominant countries) find that many of their rights, as well as their social standing, were dependent on their relationship to their husband and disappear when he is gone. In many countries their social lives, and their lives as women, are considered to be over. If they have children they are expected to dedicate themselves totally to them. However, they may also be considered "fair game" for other men or threats to other marriages and, therefore, not included in any but family gatherings.

Many widows become financially dependent on other male family members and are subject to their authority. Many of these women, both those widowed and those divorced, are financially handicapped. In some countries they are not permitted to own property of their own or to work and so have nothing to fall back on except the charity of either an ex-husband or the family of a deceased one.

Although the expatriate women may be handicapped in seeking lives of their own in the country of their ex- or deceased husbands, they may have lived so long in their adoptive country that they don't know where else to go. They may have lost track of not only old home friends but, because of the many years away, of the style of life in their homelands as well. They may feel (and with reason) that they have burned all their bridges, that they don't fit in any more. The problems of starting out again, finding a new (or their old) identity, reinserting themselves in their old world and building a new life are almost overwhelming.

Many of them find themselves alone, without jobs, without homes of their own, without true support systems, often without enough money to get by, and they don't know what to do. They feel that they have no independent identity in their adoptive countries and have lost their place in their native lands. They don't know where home is. They feel like foreigners, everywhere.

When there has been a divorce, the native spouse is normally welcomed back into the fold. If there is blame to be placed, it is generally placed on the foreigner or on the fact that the marriage was a bad idea in the first place. For many, the divorce proves that the marriage should never have taken place at all, that like should marry like, that intercultural marriage is deviant and doomed from the start, that now they should find someone of their *own* kind.

Many intercultural marriages drag on when they should end. Many poor marriages endure because it takes too much strength to end them or because it takes too much time and effort to sort the relationships out—to know when the problems are personal and when they are cultural. Many endure because of financial dependence, others out of pride. But most poor intercultural marriages endure because the partners don't know where to go if it ends.

CONCLUSION

For the vision of one person lends not its wings to another person.
—Kahlil Gibran, *The Prophet*

When a couple feels they have done just about everything they can to learn about each other and the culture into which they will be marrying, it is time to do some assessing—of each other and then of themselves. They can do this best with some very serious one-on-one discussions about their past lives and relationships, about their ideals and expectations for the marriage, and about what it is that attracts each to the other. This is not an easy process, but there are several approaches that can be tried.

Some marriage counselors have couples design "genograms," or family diagrams, which show each ones' relationship with other family members (it also shows *whom* they consider family) and how these relationships have influenced their personalities and the ways they approach life in general, and marriage in particular. This can be attempted by the partners themselves. Using circles for women and squares for men, they each begin their family trees with whomever they consider most central or important (and later discuss why) and go on from there, talking about the other people in their families, their feelings about them, and specific events they associate with each person, as these are added to the tree. Most couples will find that not only will many of their differences (personal and cultural) be exposed, but many similarities will surface regarding the kind of experiences or relationships they have— similarities which perhaps attracted them to one another without either one being consciously aware of it.[46]

It is often difficult to conceptualize exactly what one wants from life and marriage, to state expectations in so many words. For this reason some couples have drawn up premarital contracts—contracts which have nothing to do with money, but everything to do with what each wants or expects his/her life with the other to be.

Each makes a list of what is considered essential to his or her well-being whether that means going out to dinner once a week or having a maid, having a husband who is faithful or a wife with a career, having children raised in a certain faith or educated in a certain language, practicing birth control or

[46] For more on this method, see Jack O. Bradt, *The Family Diagram: Method, Technique and Use in Family Therapy,* 1980.

having a live-in mother-in-law, living in one's own country or eating one's own food, verbally communicating about difficulties and exploring possible solutions together or keeping one's feelings or problems to one's self, spending a lot of time together or requiring private space where each can have extended periods of time alone.

When the lists are complete, the couple discusses the items openly and fairly, taking turns, attempting, as much as humanly possible, to eliminate the self-seeking wants and to respect each other's needs. Finally, keeping in mind that to succeed they both need to win, the two negotiate a contract regarding how they will live together as a couple.

This process is useful not only for reaching some kind of agreement, but also as a means of exposing deeply felt needs, wants and attitudes which may not have been previously expressed. It brings out both partners' basic goals in life and for the marriage. It is a good indicator of (1) each partner's willingness to negotiate, (2) the flexibility and openness to untried (and perhaps unknown) alternatives, (3) the sensitivity to each other's needs, (4) the ability to communicate and to negotiate, and (5) the commitment to the relationship. In short, the process exposes where each one stands regarding the ten essential factors for success that we discussed earlier. It gives each partner time to see and to think about what life with this other person will be like and whether or not the differences are surmountable. It enables each one to confront the realities about each other and their relationship *before* they are legally married. People of some cultures will resist this kind of self-exposure and examining, but it offers a good opportunity for them to see what it will be like to live with someone who considers open communication essential. On the other side, it is a good time for the opposite partner to uncover the communication difficulties that lie ahead.

Another way for future spouses to explore their attitudes and goals is for each to confess why he/she *really* fell in love with the other and what it is that he/she most likes about the other. Sometimes this will expose stereotypic thinking, hidden agendas, secret weaknesses or fears.

One Japanese-Italian couple found that each of them was marrying what they expected or wanted the other to be, not what he or she really was. The Japanese girl, who thought she was getting a demonstrative, sexy Latin lover, found herself with an Italian boy who wanted separate bedrooms and couldn't bear to take her arm when they were crossing the street. He thought he was getting a docile, reserved, demurring Oriental flower who would polish his shoes and walk in his shadow, and found himself with a self-willed tiger.

This mutual "confession" is a good way of finding out whether the partners have been attracted to each other for that which each likes best about him- or herself (her independence; his machoism, etc.) or whether they are looking for qualities the other doesn't value (consigning themselves to lives devoted to frustrating attempts at transforming the other into the ideal mate). It is a good way of finding out just how each partner feels about the other's culture, whether there are hidden prejudices or ethnocentric biases which might endanger the future relationship. It is a way of getting things out in the open—of clarifying doubts, answering questions about one another and what life together will be. At this point each partner has to do some heavy self-examination, making use of all the information that has been gleaned, and decide whether or not it is possible to cope with the ambiguity, the confusion, the strain of marrying someone who possibly sees most things in a very different way.

The important thing is for each partner to find out as much as possible about the other and the other's culture *and* about themselves and their own cultural makeup *before* the wedding. It is not easy for any two people ever to really know one another, but for two who come from such different backgrounds, there are twice as many unknowns which must be flushed out and considered. It takes more effort, more time, and more honesty. It takes realizing that it is not always possible to live with a loved one, that sometimes love turns to hate if the differences are too many or too deep. It saves a lot of heartache if the partners can find this out beforehand, rather than go through the pain of separation later.

Intercultural couples have chosen a complicated route in life, one which takes more work, more empathy—more everything! They must realize this beforehand and be ready to give whatever it takes, never losing track of the fact that in the end, if all goes well, they also have the possibility of getting *more* than couples who didn't dare to be different.

BIBLIOGRAPHY

ALIREZA, Marianne. *At the Drop of a Veil*. London: Robert Hale & Co., 1971.

BARBERA, Augustin. *Mariages sans Frontieres*. Paris: Editions du Centurion, 1985.

BARRON, Milton. *The Blending American, Patterns of Intermarriage*. Chicago: Quadrangle Books, 1972.

BARZINI, Luigi. *The Italians*. New York: Atheneum, 1964.

BENEDICT, Ruth. *The Chrysanthemum and the Sword*. Boston: Houghton Mifflin, 1946.

BENEDICT, Ruth. *Patterns of Culture*. Boston: Houghton Mifflin, 1934.

BRADT, Jack O. *The Family Diagram: Method, Technique and Use in Family Therapy* Washington, DC: Groome Center, 1980.

CONDON, J.C., and Fathi Yousef. *An Introduction to Intercultural Communication*. Indianapolis, IN: Bobbs Merrill Co., 1975.

COOK, Hope. *Time Change*. New York: Simon & Schuster, 1980.

DIEKMAN, John R. *Human Connections*. Englewood Cliffs, NJ: Prentice-Hall, 1982.

DUNN, S. Kanu. "Health Seeking Behaviors and Barriers to Care among Transcultural Families." *Bridges in Health Care*. Washington, DC: Mirands Associates, 1986.

ERICKSON, Erik H. *Identity, Youth and Crisis*. New York: W.W. Norton & Co., 1968.

FAST, Julius. *Body Language*. London: Souvenir Press, 1978.

FIEG, John P., and John G. Blair. *There Is a Difference*. Washington, DC: Meridian House International, 1975.

FORER, Lucille. *The Birth Order Factor*. New York: David McKay Co., 1976.

GOLDEN, Marita. *Migrations of the Heart*. New York: Ballantine Books, Random House, 1983.

GORNICK, Vivian. *In Search of Ali Mahmoud: An American Woman in Egypt*. New York: Saturday Review Press, 1973.

HALL, Edward T. *The Dance of Life*. Garden City, NY: Anchor Press/ Doubleday, 1984.

HALL, Edward T. "Learning the Arabs' Silent Language." Reprinted from *Psychology Today*, 1979, in *The Bridge*, Spring 1980.

Ho, Man Keung. *Building a Successful Intermarriage between Religions, Social Classes, Ethnic Groups or Races*. St. Meinrad, IA: St. Meinrad Archabbey, 1984.

HORNEY, Karen. *The Neurotic Personality of Our Time*. New York: W.W. Norton & Co., 1964.

JHABVALA, Ruth Prawer. *Out of India*. New York: William Morrow & Co., 1985.

JUERGENSMEYER, Mark. *Fighting with Gandhi*. San Francisco: Harper & Row, 1984.

KINGSTON, Maxine Hong. *The Woman Warrior*. New York: Vintage Books, Random House, 1977.

KLUCKHOHN, F.R., and F.L. Strodtbeck. *Variations in Value Orientations*. Evanston: Row & Peterson, 1961.

KOCHMAN, Thomas. *Black and White Styles in Conflict*. Chicago, IL: University of Chicago Press, 1981.

KOHLS, L. Robert. *Survival Kit for Overseas Living*. Yarmouth, ME: Intercultural Press, Inc., 1984.

KURIAN, G., ed. *Cross-Cultural Perspectives of Mate Selection and Marriage*. Westport, CT: Greenwood Press, 1979.

LAMB, Patricia Frazier, and Kathryn Joyce Hohlwein. *Touchstones, Letters between Two Women, 1953-1964*. New York: Harper & Row Publishers, 1983.

LEDERER, William J. *Marital Choices*. New York: W.W. Norton & Co., 1981.

LEE, Daniel B. *Military Transcultural Marriage: A Study of Marital Adjustment between American Husbands and Korean-born Spouses*. Salt Lake City: University of Utah, Graduate School of Social Work, n.d.

MACE, D.R., and V. Mace. *Marriage East and West.* Garden City, NY: Doubleday, 1960.

MAHMOODY, Betty, with William Hoffer. *Not Without My Daughter.* New York: St. Martin's Press, 1983.

McGOLDRICK, M., John K. Pearce, and J. Giordano. *Ethnicity and Family Therapy.* New York: Guilford Family Therapy Series, Guilford Press, 1982.

MEAD, Margaret. *Male and Female, A Study of the Sexes in a Changing World.* Middlesex, England: Penguin, Pelican, 1950.

MILN, Louise Jordan. *Mr. & Mrs. Sen.* New York: Frederick A. Stokes, 1923.

MORRIS, Desmond et al. *Gestures.* New York: Stein & Day Publishers, 1979.

PALAZZOLI, M.S., L. Boscolo, G. Cecchin, and G. Prata. *Paradox and Counterparadox.* New York: Jason Aronson, Inc. (English Translation Copyright), 1978.

OLDENBURG, Don. "In One Ear...." *Washington Post.* Washington, DC: February 27, 1987.

PUSCH, Margaret D. ed. *Multicultural Education: A Cross-Cultural Training Approach.* Yarmouth, ME: Intercultural Press, Inc., 1979.

ROSEN, Steven. *Future Facts.* New York: Simon & Schuster, 1973.

SAWDEY, Michael ed. *Women in Shadows: A Handbook for Service Providers Working with Asian Wives of U.S. Military Personnel.* LaJolla, CA: National Committee Concerned with Asian Wives of U.S. Servicemen, 1981.

SCARF, Maggie. *Intimate Partners: Patterns in Love and Marriage.* New York: Random House, 1987.

STEINER, Shari. *The Female Factor: Women in Western Europe.* Yarmouth, ME: Intercultural Press, Inc., 1977.

STERN, Phyllis Noerager. *Women, Health and Culture.* New York: Hemisphere Publishing Co., McGraw Hill, 1986.

STEWART, Edward C. *American Cultural Patterns: A Cross-Cultural Perspective.* Yarmouth, ME: Intercultural Press, Inc., 1972.

TANNEN, Deborah. *That's Not What I Meant.* New York: Ballantine Books, 1986.

TOFFLER, Alvin. *Future Shock.* New York: Bantam Books, Random House, 1970.

TSENG, W.S., J.F. McDermott, and T.W. Maretzki. *Adjustment in Intercultural Marriage.* Honolulu: University of Hawaii Press, 1977.

VARRO, Gabrielle. *La Femme Transplanteé* Lilles, France: Presses Universitaires de Lilles, 1984.

WERKMAN, Sidney. *Bringing Up Children Overseas.* New York: Basic Books, 1977.

WOLFGANG, Aaron ed. *Nonverbal Behavior, Perspectives, Applications, Intercultural Insights.* Lewiston, NY: Hogrefe, Inc., 1984.